面朝大海

春暖花开

QINHUANGDAO

这
就是
《这就是秦皇岛》编委会

编著

秦皇岛

燕山大学出版社

·秦皇岛·

图书在版编目（CIP）数据

这就是秦皇岛 / 《这就是秦皇岛》编委会编著.

秦皇岛 ： 燕山大学出版社，2025. 3. -- ISBN 978-7
-5761-0795-1

Ⅰ．K922.23

中国国家版本馆 CIP 数据核字第 2024S71N59 号

这就是秦皇岛
ZHE JIU SHI QINHUANGDAO

《这就是秦皇岛》编委会 编著

出 版 人：陈　玉

责任编辑：王　宁

责任印制：吴　波　　　　　　　封面设计：吴　波

出版发行：燕山大学出版社　　　电　　话：0335-8387555

地　　址：河北省秦皇岛市河北大街西段 438 号　　邮政编码：066004

印　　刷：秦皇岛墨缘彩印有限公司　　经　　销：全国新华书店

开　本：889 mm×1194 mm　　1/16　　印　次：18

版　次：2025 年 3 月第 1 版　　印　次：2025 年 3 月第 1 次印刷

书　号：ISBN 978-7-5761-0795-1　　字　数：180 千字

定　价：198.00 元　　审 图 号：冀秦 S（2025）001 号

Qin
huang
dao

　　从北京驱车一路向东，来到渤海岸边，一脚踏进沙滩，清澈海水与碧蓝天空，映衬着孤独图书馆和白色的礼堂，每一处都让人流连忘返。这就是秦皇岛的阿那亚了。

　　这里，大海、设计独到的建筑、文艺的生活方式，成为年轻人追慕的网红艺术打卡地，赋予了这座城市无尽的诗意和美好。

　　走进秦皇岛，不仅看到这里的自然禀赋、过往历史与今朝故事，还将看到新的城市和新兴产业的蓬勃兴起，它们在新赛道上，如大潮奔涌，生生不息。

Driving east from Beijing to the shores of the Bohai Sea, you step onto the sandy beach, where the crystal-clear waters and azure skies frame the iconic Lonely Library and the pristine white chapel. Every corner of this place leaves an unforgettable impression. This is Aranya, Qinhuangdao.

Here, the sea, the uniquely designed architecture, and the artistic way of life have made it a sought-after destination for young people, a hotspot for art and culture. It imbues the city with endless poetry and beauty.

Stepping into Qinhuangdao, you will not only witness its natural gifts, its rich history, and its present-day stories, but also the rise of a new city and thriving emerging industries. Like a surging tide, they are forging ahead on new paths, full of vitality and endless momentum.

目 CONTENTS 录

Qinhuangdao

THIS IS

初识秦皇岛
面朝大海的一座城

FIRST IMPRESSION OF QINHUANGDAO
A CITY FACING THE SEA

这就是秦皇岛
THIS IS QINHUANGDAO

公元前 215 年，
千古一帝秦始皇东巡至此，
刻《碣石门辞》，
并派人入海求仙。
她由此得名，
是中国唯一以皇帝名号命名的城市。
这就是秦皇岛。

秦皇岛钟灵毓秀、名胜荟萃，
风光绮丽、气候宜人，
是国家历史文化名城、
中国首批优秀旅游城市、
河北省零距离滨海城市，
素有"长城滨海公园"
"京津后花园"的美誉。

2017 年成功创建全国文明城市，
2018 年成功创建国家森林城市，
2021 年成功创建国家卫生城市，
2023 年荣获中国人居环境奖综合奖。

In 215 BC, Qin Shi Huang, the First Emperor of China, journeyed east to this land. He inscribed the Jieshi Gate Inscription and sent envoys to sea in search of immortality. It was from this legendary event that the city derived its name, making it the only city in China named after an emperor. This is Qinhuangdao.

Qinhuangdao is a place of natural beauty and cultural richness, where stunning landscapes and a pleasant climate converge. As a nationally renowned historical and cultural city, it is among the first excellent tourist cities. It is the city in Hebei Province directly bordering the coast. Known as the "Great Wall Coastal Park" and the "Back Garden of Beijing and Tianjin", it has long been celebrated for its charm.

In 2017, it was recognized as a National Civilized City. In 2018, it earned the title of National Forest City. In 2021, it was designated a National Sanitary City. And in 2023, it was honored with the Comprehensive Award of China's Habitat Environment Award.

陆域面积
7802 平方公里

海域面积
1805 平方公里

常住人口
311.14 万人

秦皇岛下辖海港区、北戴河区、山海关区、抚宁区，
昌黎县、卢龙县、青龙满族自治县
和秦皇岛经济技术开发区、北戴河新区。

Qinhuangdao administers the Haigang District, Beidaihe District, Shanhaiguan District, Funing District, Changli County, Lulong County, Manchu Autonomous County of Qinglong, as well as the Qinhuangdao Economic and Technological Development Zone and Beidaihe New Area.

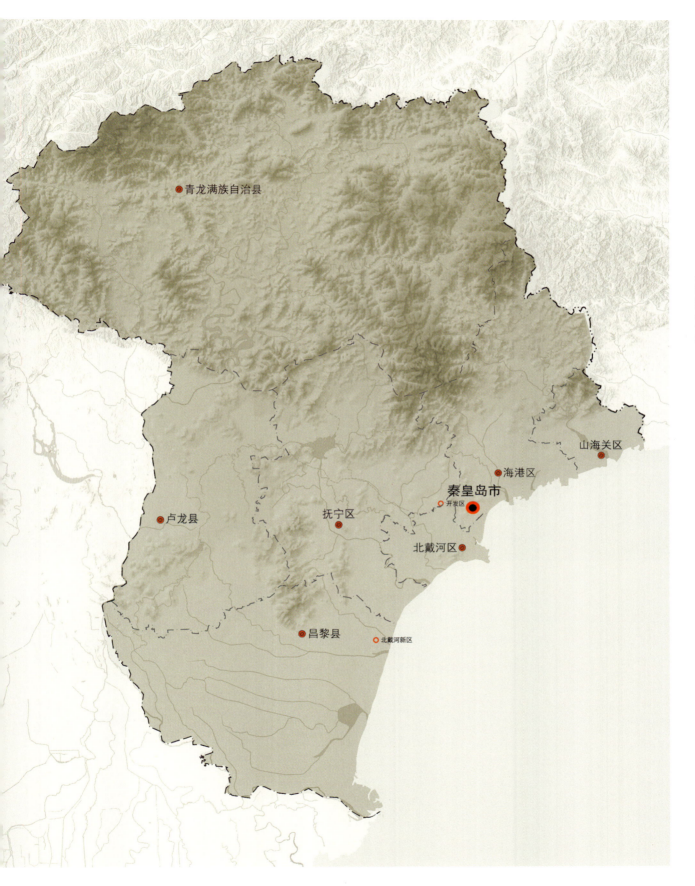

青龙满族自治县

山海关区

海港区

秦皇岛市

开发区

卢龙县

抚宁区

北戴河区

昌黎县

北戴河新区

秦皇岛
是中国首批沿海开放城市

Qinhuangdao was among China's first coastal open cities

1984 年，
秦皇岛被国务院批准为全国首批沿海开放城市。
同年，经国务院批准成立秦皇岛经济技术开发区，
是全国首批国家级经济技术开发区之一。
秦皇岛凭借优质开放平台，
吸引了 57 个国家和地区的客商投资置业，
被评为"中国外贸百强城市"。
秦皇岛综合保税区同时享有保税区、
保税物流园区和出口加工区相关的税收和外汇管理政策，
2022 年在全国综保区发展绩效评估中进入"双 B"序列。

In 1984, Qinhuangdao was approved by the State Council as one of the initial coastal open cities. In the same year, the Qinhuangdao Economic and Technological Development Zone was established with State Council approval, also being among the first national-level economic and technological development zones. This high-quality open platform has attracted investors and businesses from 57 countries and regions, earning Qinhuangdao one of "China's Top 100 Foreign Trade Cities". The Qinhuangdao Comprehensive Bonded Zone enjoys tax and foreign exchange management policies related to bonded zones, bonded logistics parks, and export processing zones. In 2022, it entered the "Double B" sequence in the national evaluation of bonded zone development performance.

| 浪漫家园 |
| Haven of Romance |

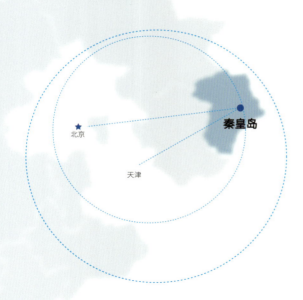

秦皇岛

北京

天津

秦皇岛
是京津冀地区重要的节点城市

Qinhuangdao is an important hub city in the Beijing-Tianjin-Hebei region

秦皇岛位于河北省东北部，

南临渤海，

北依燕山，

东接辽宁，

西近京津，

地处华北、东北两大经济区接合部，

居环渤海经济圈中心地带，

是京津冀经济圈中一颗璀璨的明珠。

Located in the northeast of Hebei Province, Qinhuangdao borders the Bohai Sea to the south, is surrounded by the Yanshan Mountains to the north, connects to Liaoning to the east, and is close to Beijing and Tianjin to the west. It is situated at the junction of the North China and Northeast China economic zones, at the center of the Bohai Rim Economic Circle, known as a gorgeous pearl in the Beijing-Tianjin-Hebei Economic Circle.

| 渤海明珠 |
| Pearl of the Bohai Sea |

| 花园式港口 |
| Garden-style Port |

秦皇岛
是现代海洋城市

Qinhuangdao is a modern marine city

秦皇岛海洋资源丰富，

拥有绵长的海岸线

和完整的海洋生态系统。

秦皇岛以建设国家海洋经济、

创新发展示范城市为抓手，

向海发展、向海图强，

统筹海洋生态环境保护、

海洋资源综合利用、

海洋经济创新发展，

大力发展海洋交通运输、海洋工程装备、

海上风电光伏、海洋文化旅游和临港产业，

海洋经济呈现蓬勃发展态势。

Qinhuangdao boasts abundant marine resources, with an extensive coastline and a complete marine ecosystem. Boosting its marine economic development and leveraging its role as a national demonstration city, Qinhuangdao is striving to strengthen and expand its maritime capabilities. Qinhuangdao is striving to strengthen and expand its maritime capabilities. It balances the protection of marine ecosystems, the comprehensive utilization of marine resources, and the innovative growth of its marine economy. The city is vigorously developing marine transportation, marine engineering equipment, offshore wind and solar power, marine cultural tourism, and port-related industries. Its marine economy is now thriving with remarkable momentum.

| 美丽港湾 |
| Harbor of Serenity |

秦皇岛
是全国性综合交通枢纽城市

Qinhuangdao is a national comprehensive transport Hub

秦皇岛域内 5 条国铁和 8 条高速纵横交错，
拥有秦皇岛站、北戴河站、山海关站 3 座高铁站，
北戴河机场通达国内 13 座城市。
随着京唐秦城际铁路和京秦第二高速、
京秦高速卢新支线相继通车，
秦皇岛正加快构建多式联运的立体大交通格局，
深度融入京津"1 小时交通圈"。

Qinhuangdao is crisscrossed by 5 national railways and 8 highways, with 3 high-speed rail stations: Qinhuangdao Station, Beidaihe Station, and Shanhaiguan Station. Beidaihe Airport connects to 13 cities in China. With the opening of the Jing-Tang-Qin Intercity Railway, the second Jing-Qin Expressway, and the Lulong-Beidaihe New Area branch of the Jing-Qin Expressway, Qinhuangdao is accelerating the construction of a multi-modal transport system and is deeply integrating into the Beijing-Tianjin "1-hour transport circle".

璀璨港城
| A Radiant Port City |

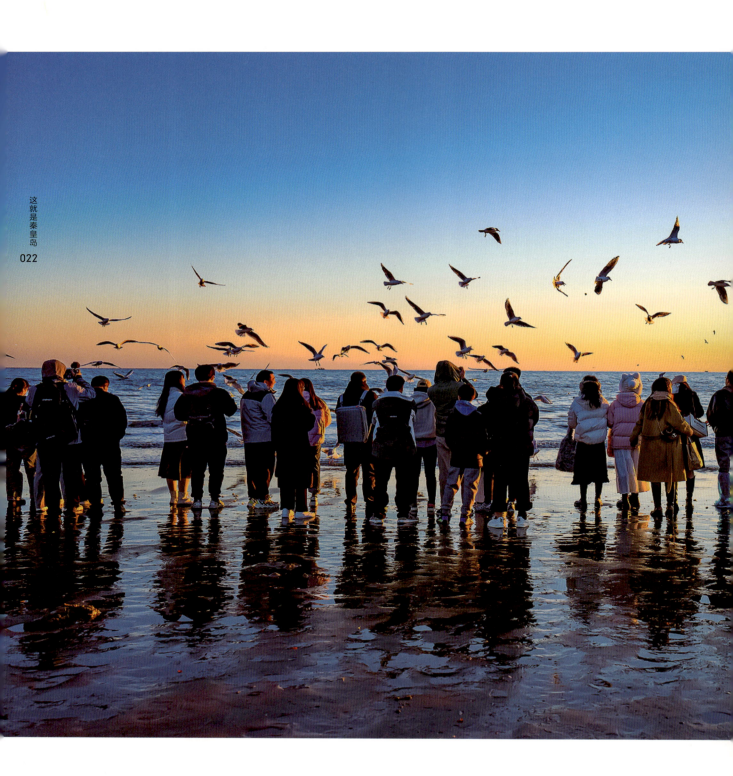

秦皇岛
是全国滨海旅游目的地

Qinhuangdao is a national coastal tourist destination

1898 年，

北戴河被辟为允许中外人士杂居的避暑地。

这里诞生了中国第一条旅游铁路专线、

第一条航空旅游航线、

第一个 19 孔高尔夫球场。

这里四季宜游，

处处皆景，

每年吸引 9000 万人次中外游客。

秦皇岛成功上榜 2024 亚洲 TOP100 旅游目的地，

入选 2024 最具潜力文旅城市。

In 1898, Beidaihe was established as a summer resort open to both Chinese and foreign nationals. It witnessed the creation of China's first dedicated tourist railway line, the first air tourism route, and the country's inaugural 19-hole golf course. Qinhuangdao is a year-round travel destination, offering scenic spots in every season. The city attracts 90 million visitors from both China and abroad each year. It was named one of the top 100 tourist destinations in Asia in 2024 and selected as one of the most promising cultural tourism cities of 2024.

北戴河

Beidaihe

北戴河是驰名中外的"夏都"，
是中国近现代旅游发源地，
还是首批国家级重点风景名胜区、
首批中国优秀旅游城市、
首批国家全域旅游示范区。

Beidaihe, renowned domestically and internationally as the "Summer Capital" , is the birthplace of tourism in China. It is among the first national key scenic and historic areas, the first batch of China's Excellent Tourist Cities, and the first national All-Area Tourism Demonstration Zones.

鸽子窝公园
湿地平整开阔。
海边天然高地上建有日出亭，
视野极佳，
是观赏日出的绝佳点位。
天气晴朗时，
游客能在此处欣赏到红日跃出海面的震撼景象。
鸽子窝公园以"观沧海、近万鸟、赏日出、看大潮坪、
访伟人足迹"驰名国内外。

The wetland of Geziwo Park is flat and expansive, and a natural highland by the sea hosts a pavilion for sunrise viewing. It offers an excellent vantage point for watching the sunrise, where visitors can enjoy the stunning sight of the sun rising from the sea on clear days. Geziwo Park is famous both at home and abroad for its "Viewing the Cang Sea, Approaching Thousands of Birds, Enjoying the Sunrise, Observing the Great Tide Flats, and Visiting the Footprints of Great Figures".

| 鸽子窝公园 |
| Geziwo Park |

| 老虎石公园 |
| Laohushi Park |

老虎石公园

是北戴河旅游旺季海浴人数最多的浴场，

海水水质优良，

环境清幽，

碧海、金沙、礁石独具特色，

如镶嵌在渤海之滨的一颗明珠，

闪烁着璀璨的光辉，

以绚丽多姿的面貌，

迎接着中外游客。

Laohushi Park is the busiest beach during the peak tourist season in Beidaihe. The water quality is excellent, and the environment is serene. With its unique combination of clear blue seas, golden sands, and distinctive rocks, it sparkles like a pearl by the Bohai Sea, welcoming visitors from all over the world with vibrant and ever-changing scenery.

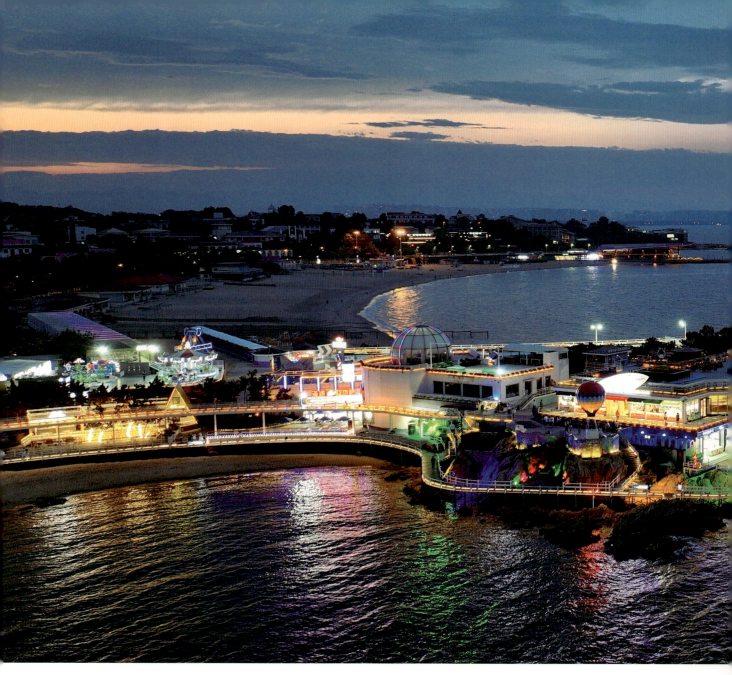

| 碧螺塔海上酒吧公园 |
| Biluota Bar Park |

碧螺塔海上酒吧公园

位于北戴河海滨最东侧，

园内主建筑碧螺塔为海滨东山地区最高点，

塔高 21 米，共 7 层，

是世界上独一无二的海螺形螺旋观光塔。

登塔远眺，"秦皇岛外打鱼船"的海上风光尽收眼底。

游客在此早观日出，晚看篝火，其乐融融……

The Biluota Bar Park is located at the easternmost edge of Beidaihe's coastline. The park's main building, the Biluota Tower, is the tallest structure in the Eastern Mountain area of Beidaihe, standing 21 meters tall and consisting of 7 levels. It is a unique, spiral seashell-shaped observation tower. From the top of the tower, visitors can enjoy panoramic views of the "fishing boats outside Qinhuangdao" and the surrounding seascape. Tourists come here to watch the sunrise in the morning and enjoy bonfires in the evening, creating a joyful and harmonious atmosphere.

| 吴家楼（吴鼎昌别墅）|
| Wujia Lou (Wu Dingchang Villa) |

北戴河近代别墅群

属滨海型建筑群，

涵盖国家、省、市（县、区）

三级文物保护单位。

目前尚有 94 栋老别墅建筑，

集世界建筑风格之大成，

记录了中国近现代史的风云变幻。

The modern villa clusters in Beidaihe, categorized as coastal architectural complexes, encompass cultural heritage sites protected at the national, provincial, and municipal (county/district) levels. Currently preserving 94 historic villas, these structures epitomize a synthesis of global architectural styles while bearing witness to the sweeping transformations of China's modern and contemporary history.

| 东金草燕（何香凝）别墅 |
| Soen Togane (He Xiangning Villa) |

| 雷尔别墅 |
| Lei'er Villa |

| 阿温太太别墅 |
| Madame Aweng's Villa |

| 章家楼（章瑞庭别墅）|
| Zhangjia Lou (Zhang Ruiting Villa) |

山海关
Shanhaiguan

山海关
是享誉世界的历史文化名城，
是世界文化遗产地。
其以雄伟独特的风姿屹立在渤海之滨，
素有"两京锁钥无双地，万里长城第一关"的美誉。

老龙头
是明长城的东部入海处，
也是万里长城建设体系中
唯一一处海陆一体军事防御设施。
今天的老龙头以旖旎的渤海风光、
独特的园林景色、
伟奇的长城，
向人们展示了其独特的文物价值、
考古价值、旅游价值，
成为闻名遐迩的风景名胜旅游区。

Shanhaiguan is a world-renowned historical and cultural city and a UNESCO World Heritage site. It stands majestically at the shores of the Bohai Sea, earning the nickname "The Key to the Two Capitals and the First Pass of the Great Wall".

Laolongtou (Old Dragon Head) served as the eastern terminus of the Great Wall where it meets the sea, standing as the sole integrated land-and-sea military defense structure within the Ming Dynasty's Great Wall construction system. Today, Laolongtou showcases its unique archaeological, historical, and touristic value with its picturesque Bohai Sea views, distinctive gardens, and magnificent Great Wall, making it a renowned scenic spot.

天下第一关

是明长城的重要关隘之一，

素有中国长城"三大奇观之一"、

"边郡之咽喉，京师之保障"之称。

著名的"天下第一关"匾额，

书法雄劲有力，

与城楼浑然一体，

大有镇关之风，

为关口增添了威严和气势，

堪称古今巨作。

山海关古城

与长城相连，

以城为关。

城内钟鼓楼、古街巷、兵部分司署等

建筑保存完好，

不仅展示了中国古代严密的城防建筑风格，

还充分展现了山海关这座古代军事要塞

"一夫当关，万夫莫开"的雄伟气势。

The First Pass of the World is one of important gates of the Ming Great Wall, known as one of the "Three Great Wonders of the Great Wall of China" and dubbed the "Throat of Border Counties and the Guard of the Capital". The famous "First Pass of the World" plaque, with its strong and powerful calligraphy, blends seamlessly with the city gate, adding to its grandeur and authority, making it a remarkable masterpiece of ancient and modern times.

The ancient city of Shanhaiguan is connected to the Great Wall, serving as a gateway. Structures such as bell and drum towers, ancient streets, and military offices are well-preserved, showcasing the meticulous city defense architectural style of ancient China and demonstrating the grandeur of this military stronghold, where the saying "one man guarding the pass can hold back ten thousand" truly comes to life.

| 老龙头 |
| Laolongtou |

天下第一关
| The First Pass of the World |

| 山海关古城 |
| The Ancient City of Shanhaiguan |

阿那亚
Aranya

阿那亚

位于北戴河新区，

社区内有如马尔代夫般的海边风景，

有海滩酒吧，

有世界上最孤独的图书馆，

还有最浪漫的海边礼堂。

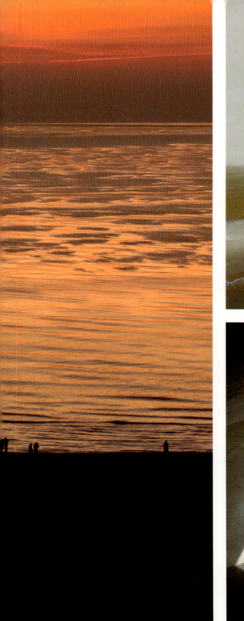

Aranya is located in the Beidaihe New Area, offering a seaside landscape akin to the Maldives. It features beach bars, the world's loneliest library, and the most romantic seaside chapel.

西港花园
Xigang Garden

西港花园

位于海港区，

由秦皇岛港西港区工业遗迹焕新而生。

这里既不乏独有的工业氛围和深厚底蕴，

又充满海港味道和时尚气息，

尽展百年港区的时代芳华，

正着力创建国家 5A 级旅游景区。

Xigang Garden is located in the Haigang District, transformed from the industrial relics of the western port area of Qinhuangdao Port. The area blends a unique industrial atmosphere and deep historical roots with a strong maritime vibe and a fashionable flair, showcasing the century-old port's vibrancy. It is currently focused on developing a national 5A-level tourism attraction.

天女小镇
Tian Nv Town

天女小镇

位于海港区石门寨镇，

围绕"山地康养、四季体验"的主题进行打造。

小镇融入生态康养、运动康养、禅修康养等新业态，

呼应海上度假游船与祖山风景区，

将"海上游"与"山林游"衔接，

将一季游延伸为四季游。

Tian Nv Town is located in Shimen Zhai Town, Haigang District. It is built around the theme of "mountain wellness and four-season experiences". The town integrates new activities such as ecological wellness, sports wellness, and meditation wellness, complementing maritime tourism and the Mount Zu Scenic Area. It combines "sea tours" with "mountain and forest tours", extending seasonal tourism into a year-round experience.

蔚蓝海岸
Seatopia

蔚蓝海岸

位于北戴河新区，

是滨海休闲度假大型旅游综合体，

拥有中国帆船帆板运动协会北方总部基地、

儿童主题乐园、猫的天空之城概念书店。

Seatopia, nestled within the Beidaihe New District, stands as a grand coastal resort complex that epitomizes leisure and recreation. It proudly hosts the northern headquarters of the Chinese Sailing Association, a whimsical children's theme park, and the renowned Momicafe bookstore.

渔田小镇
Yutian Town

渔田小镇

位于北戴河新区，

紧邻七里海潟湖湿地，

是集夜游演艺、沉浸式体验街区、

渔文化精粹、特色民宿集群、

亲子研学、温泉康养于一体的

全新型一站式旅游度假目的地。

Yutian Town, situated in the Beidaihe New Area adjacent to the Qilihai Lagoon Wetland, is an all-new, one-stop tourist resort destination that integrates night performances, immersive experience neighborhoods, refined fishing culture, clusters of unique homestays, parent-child educational studies, and hot spring service.

渔岛
Yu Island Resort

渔岛
位于北戴河新区，
景区内遍布 12 个沙湖，
湖水清澈见底。
景区内不仅能够温泉泡澡，
还能观赏大海的美景，
游客在此可以体验"泡着温泉看大海"的
浪漫情调。

Yu Island Resort, located in the Beidaihe New Area, features twelve sandy lakes with crystal-clear waters. Visitors can soak in hot springs while enjoying views of the ocean, offering a romantic experience of "soaking in hot springs while watching the sea".

如是海
Resea

如是海
位于北戴河新区，
拥有大海、沙滩、森林、湖泊、温泉等
珍稀的自然资源，
森林覆盖率高达 75%。
这里是集吃、住、游、娱、购于一体的
滨海高端隐奢度假目的地，
为追求高品质度假体验的游客提供了
一个远离喧嚣、亲近自然的理想之选。

Resea, located on the Beidaihe New Area, is a high-end,
exclusive coastal resort that boasts rare natural resources
such as the sea, beaches, forests, lakes, and hot springs,
with a forest coverage rate of 75%. It offers an all-in-one
experience of dining, lodging, entertainment, shopping,
and relaxation, making it an ideal choice for travelers
seeking a luxurious, peaceful escape close to nature.

秦皇岛野生动物园
Qinhuangdao Safari Park

秦皇岛野生动物园
位于北戴河海滨国家森林公园内，
占地面积 3500 余亩。
园区利用林海、绿地模拟各种动物的原生环境，
放养着 120 余种来自世界各地的珍禽名兽，
目前正在建设大熊猫馆。

Qinhuangdao Safari Park, located within the Beidaihe Coastal National Forest Park, covers an area of over 3,500 acres. The park utilizes forests and green spaces to mimic the natural habitats of various animals, housing over 120 rare and magnificent species from around the world. A panda pavilion is currently under construction.

跌宕三千年

历史在此风云际会

THREE MILLENNIA OF TUMULTUOUS HISTORY
WHERE HISTORY UNFOLDS DRAMATICALLY

这就是秦皇岛
THIS IS QINHUANGDAO

"江山代有才人出，

各领风骚数百年。"

秦皇岛历史文化底蕴厚重，

有文字记载的人类文明史可以追溯至

3600 多年前的商代孤竹国。

三千多载的岁月长河，

留下了夷齐让国、始皇驻跸、

戚继光驻守边关等经典故事。

"Every age breeds its heroes, each reigning in glory for centuries." The history of Qinhuangdao is rich and profound, with recorded human civilization dating back to the Shang Dynasty's Guzhu State, more than 3,600 years ago. Over the course of these three millennia, many classical stories have emerged, including the benevolent rule of Yi and Qi, Emperor Qin Shi Huang's visits, and General Qi Jiguang's defense of the frontier. Countless emperors, heroes, revolutionaries, and scholars have left behind their legacies, writing timeless masterpieces that continue to be celebrated today, adding vibrant depth to the city.

史话孤竹

The History of Guzhu

商汤灭夏建立商朝，

封孤竹君，立孤竹国。

据唐人李泰所编《括地志》记载：

"孤竹故城在平州卢龙县南十二里，殷时诸侯孤竹国也。"

商时秦皇岛地区便属孤竹国。

伯夷、叔齐二人为商末孤竹国君之子。

夷齐二人"兄弟让国、叩马而谏、耻食周粟、首阳采薇"的

仁哲大义流传千古，

是历代中华仁人志士诚信礼让、抱节守志的典范。

The Shang Dynasty's King Tang overthrew the Xia Dynasty and established the Shang Dynasty, appointing the ruler of Guzhu and founding the Guzhu State. According to Li Tai's *Kuodizhi* in the Tang Dynasty: "The ruins of Guzhu are located twelve miles south of Lulong County in Pingzhou; Guzhu was a vassal state during the Shang Dynasty." During the Shang period, the Qinhuangdao region was part of the Guzhu State. The two historical figures, Bo Yi and Shu Qi, were the sons of the ruler of Guzhu. The brothers Bo Yi and Shu Qi are famous for their noble virtues, such as their willingness to abdicate the throne, stopping emperor's horse to give counsel, rejecting the food from the Zhou dynasty, and feeding on bracken on Mount Shouyang. Their story has been passed down through the ages as an example of integrity, humility, and adherence to one's principles.

| 秦夔龙纹大瓦当 |
| Qin "Kui-long" Pattern Large Eaves Tile (Wadang) |

始皇驻跸

Emperor Qin's Visit

公元前 221 年，

秦始皇统一六国。

出于安定疆土、巩固统一、宣示国威的政治目的，

秦始皇进行了 5 次大规模巡行。

公元前 215 年，

秦始皇第四次出巡，

到达地处渤海之滨的碣石，

并在这里修建了大规模的行宫建筑群。

In 221 BC, Qin Shi Huang conquered the six warring states. For the purpose of stabilizing his borders, consolidating unity, and demonstrating his national power, Emperor Qin Shi Huang embarked on five major tours. In 215 BC, he made his fourth tour, reaching Jieshi by the Bohai Sea, where he built a grand palace complex.

| 北戴河秦行宫遗址 |
| Beidaihe Qin Dynasty Palace Ruins |

东临碣石

Passing by Mount Jieshi

东汉建安十二年（207 年），
曹操挥鞭北指，率军讨伐乌桓，道出卢龙塞。
是年深秋，乌桓授首，
曹操率大军沿辽西走廊班师回朝，
途经碣石，观海赋诗，
留下千古绝唱《观沧海》。

In the 12th year of the Jian'an era in the Eastern Han Dynasty (207 CE), Cao Cao led his northern expedition against the Wuhuan tribes, advancing through the Longshan Pass. That late autumn, after decisively defeating the Wuhuan forces, his triumphant army marched back along the Liaoxi Corridor. Passing by Jieshi (a coastal landmark near present-day Qinhuangdao), Cao Cao gazed upon the sea and composed his poetic masterpiece "Viewing the Vast Sea" (Guan Canghai).

| 东临碣石　以观沧海 |
| Climbing Jieshi's Eastern Cliffs　To Viewing the Vast Sea |

太宗赋诗

Emperor Taizong's Poem

唐贞观十九年（645 年），

唐太宗东征高句丽。

据《旧唐书•太宗本纪》记载：

"冬十月丙辰，入临渝关，

皇太子自定州迎谒。

戊午，次汉武台，刻石以纪功德。"

据《资治通鉴》记载：

"临渝关，在柳城西四百八十里，所谓卢龙之险也。"

唐太宗李世民在这里写下一首《春日望海》，

其中有诗句："之罘思汉帝，碣石想秦皇。"

In the 19th year of the Zhenguan reign in the Tang Dynasty (645 AD), Emperor Taizong of Tang launched a military campaign against Goguryeo. According to the *Taizongbenji in Old Tang History*: "In the tenth month of winter, the crown prince met him at Linyu Pass, and they carved stone to commemorate the achievements." *The Comprehensive Mirror to Aid in Government* records: "Linyu Pass is 480 miles west of Liucheng, known for its treacherous terrain." At this place, Emperor Taizong wrote the poem "Spring Day by the Sea", in which he wrote: "I think of the Han Emperor by the sea, and I recall Qin Shi Huang at Jieshi."

In the 14th year of the Hongwu era in the Ming Dynasty (1381 CE), General Xu Da was commissioned under imperial decree to fortify 32 strategic passes including Yongping and Jieling, aiming to defend against remnant Mongol forces in the north. In that year, the central military administration established the Shanhai Garrison Command-a frontier defense stronghold. Through successive expansions during the reigns of Hongwu, Yongle, Chenghua, Longqing, Wanli, and Chongzhen emperors, this evolved into an unparalleled military defense network: seven interconnected fortress cities interwoven with the Great Wall, forming an integrated defense system harmonizing mountains, sea, passes, and fortified cities.

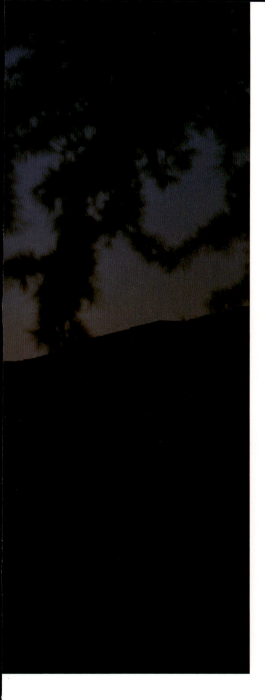

建关设卫

Establishing Passes and Garrisons

明洪武十四年（1381 年），

为防御北方的蒙古残余势力，

大将军徐达奉旨修永平、界岭等三十二关，

同年，又设置了隶属于中央军事系统的卫所"山海卫"。

历经洪武、永乐、成化、隆庆、万历、崇祯等朝不断补充修筑，

最终建成了"七城连环，长城贯穿"，

集山、海、关、城于一体的军事城防系统。

板厂峪窑址群是明代长城建筑材料烧制、兵器制造和后勤保障的重地。目前已探明各类窑址 130 余座。

The Banchangyu Kiln Site Complex served as a crucial hub for the production of building materials, weaponry, and logistical support for the Great Wall during the Ming Dynasty. To date, more than 130 kiln sites of various types have been identified.

固海筑防

Strengthening Coastal Defense

明隆庆二年（1568 年）至万历十二年（1584 年），

戚继光驻守蓟镇 16 年间，

整顿边防，修筑长城，

边备修饬，蓟镇安然。

戚继光加固了蓟镇原有的边墙，

在长城上大规模修建空心敌台，

增筑南海口入海石城七丈，

建成完备的防御工事体系，

大大完善了长城的防御功能。

From the 2nd year of the Longqing era in the Ming Dynasty (1568 CE) to the 12th year of the Wanli era (1584 CE), during his 16-year tenure as commander of the Jizhou Garrison, General Qi Jiguang reorganized frontier defenses and reinforced the Great Wall, establishing comprehensive border security that ensured the region's stability. He strengthened existing fortifications, constructed numerous hollow watchtowers along the Great Wall, and extended the Nanhai Sea Entrance by seven zhang (approximately 23 meters), creating an integrated defense system that significantly enhanced the Great Wall's military capabilities.

| 明长城纪事碑拓片 |

| Rubbing of the Ming Great Wall Chronicle Stele |

| 入海石城 |
| Stone Fortress at the Sea Entrance |

明清易鼎

The Ming and Qing Dynasties Transition

1644 年，

是农历甲申年。

李自成的农民起义军攻克北京，

统治中国 276 年的大明王朝宣告灭亡。

同年 5 月，

李自成对山海关吴三桂所部发起猛攻，

双方激战一日后，

吴三桂迎清军入关。

清军向起义军发起进攻。

起义军猝不及防，一路溃退，

李自成率部退至永平。

清军自山海关入关南下，

迅速摧毁了起义军建立的大顺政权。

同年，清顺治帝在北京登基，

清王朝的统治由此开始。

The year 1644, the year of the Jia Shen (the 12th year of the Chinese calendar).
The peasant army led by Li Zicheng captured Beijing, bringing an end to the
276-year rule of the Ming Dynasty. In May, Li Zicheng's forces launched a
fierce attack on Shanhaiguan, where Wu Sangui's troops settled. After a day
of fierce battle, Wu Sangui opened the gates to allow the Qing army to enter
the pass. The Qing forces attacked the peasant army, which was caught off
guard and retreated rapidly. Li Zicheng's forces retreated to Yongping. The
Qing army moved south from Shanhaiguan and quickly dismantled the peasant
regime, which had been established by the rebels. Later that same year, Qing
Shunzhi Emperor ascended the throne in Beijing, marking the beginning of the
Qing Dynasty's rule.

1644 年，改变中国历史走向的"甲申之战"就发生在石河流域。

In 1644, the pivotal "Jiashen Battle" that altered the course of Chinese history unfolded in the Shihe River basin.

| 石河湿地公园 |
| Shihe Wetland Park |

博物馆之城

The City of Museums

秦皇岛城市的厚重历史和记忆，
积累沉淀形成了山海关中国长城博物馆、
秦皇岛博物馆、秦皇岛市玻璃博物馆、
北戴河秦行宫遗址博物馆、电力博物馆、
秦皇岛柳江地学博物馆、港口博物馆等 24 座博物馆。

这些博物馆无论是历史遗迹的展示，
还是专题知识的普及，
都详尽地记录了秦皇岛的历史变迁，
充分展示了这座城市的独特魅力。
它们不仅极大地丰富了秦皇岛的文化内涵，
更为市民和游客提供了一个个
深入了解这座城市历史文化的窗口。

The rich history and memories of Qinhuangdao have accumulated over time, forming a collection of 24 museums, including Shanhaiguan Museum of the Great Wall of China, Qinhuangdao Museum, Qinhuangdao Museum of Glass, Beidaihe Qin Dynasty Palace Ruins, Qinhuangdao Electric Power Museum, Qinhuangdao Liujiang Geoscien Museum, and Qinhuangdao Port Museum. These museums, whether showcasing historical relics or promoting specialized knowledge, meticulously record the changes in Qinhuangdao's history, fully showcasing the unique charm of the city. They have greatly enriched the cultural depth of Qinhuangdao, providing both residents and visitors with an access into the city's historical and cultural heritage.

山海关中国长城博物馆
Shanhaiguan Museum of the Great Wall of China

山海关中国长城博物馆

作为长城国家文化公园标志性项目，

是全国唯一的长城主题国家一级博物馆。

"长城历史文化展""山海关长城展"

"长城国家文化公园规划和红色长城展"

"长城非遗展"4 个基本陈列，

相互呼应、相得益彰，

形成了一个宏观与微观完美融合的展览体系，

展示了中国长城厚重的历史文化积淀。

The Shanhaiguan Museum of the Great Wall of China is a flagship project of the Great Wall National Cultural Park and is the only national first-class museum dedicated to the Great Wall theme in the country. It features four core exhibitions: "History and Culture of the Great Wall", "Shanhaiguan Great Wall" ,"Planning of the Great Wall National Cultural Park and the Red Great Wall", and "Intangible Cultural Heritage of the Great Wall". These exhibitions complement each other, forming a perfect integration of macro and micro perspectives and showcasing the rich historical and cultural heritage of the Great Wall.

| 清乾隆景泰蓝象 |
| Cloisonné Elephant (Qianlong Reign, Qing Dynasty) |

秦皇岛博物馆
Qinhuangdao Museum

秦皇岛博物馆是一座全面展示
秦皇岛历史文化的综合性博物馆。
其主题展览"海岳明珠"，
展品丰富、传承明晰，
精练而突出地呈现了不同时期
秦皇岛独特的地域文化和城市精神，
犹如一条纽带，
串联起秦皇岛地区浩瀚而又厚重的历史。

Qinhuangdao Museum is a comprehensive museum that fully presents the history and culture of the city. Its thematic exhibition, "The Pearl of Sea and Mountain", offers a rich and clear lineage of exhibits, highlighting the unique regional culture and city spirit of Qinhuangdao at different historical periods, serving as a bridge that connects the vast and profound history of the Qinhuangdao area.

秦皇岛市玻璃博物馆
Qinhuangdao Museum of Glass

北戴河秦行宫遗址博物馆

Beidaihe Qin Dynasty Palace Ruins

电力博物馆

Electric Power Museum

秦皇岛柳江地学博物馆
Qinhuangdao Liujiang Geoscien Museum

港口博物馆
Port Museum

燕山大学东北亚古丝路文明博物馆
Yanshan University Northeast Asian Silk Road Civilization Museum

秦皇岛鸟类博物馆

Qinhuangdao Bird Museum

叁

山海灵秀地

大自然厚爱的地方

MAJESTIC MOUNTAINS AND SEAS
A LAND BLESSED BY NATURE

这就是秦皇岛

THIS IS QINHUANGDAO

秦皇岛山清水秀、天蓝海碧，

大海、沙滩、浅山、森林、湿地、温泉等资源富集，

得天独厚的自然环境，

使其成为山海灵秀之地。

好山、好水、好风光，

秦皇岛如诗如画的秀美景色令人沉醉。

Qinhuangdao is blessed with clear mountains and waters with rich resources of sea, sand, shallow mountains, forests, wetlands, and hot springs, an exceptional natural environment, making it a place of natural beauty. With beautiful mountains, waters, and scenery, the poetic and picturesque scenery of Qinhuangdao captivates visitors.

秦皇岛因海而灵

Qinhuangdao's Vitality Lies in the Sea

1805 平方公里的大海碧波荡漾，
185 公里的砂质岸线绵延旖旎。
远看秦皇岛的海，
白浪茫茫与天连，
平沙浩浩似无边。
走近浅海岸边，
海鸥群集在沙滩上，
宛如一幅幅剪影。

The vast 1,805 square kilometers of the sea ripple with clear waves, and the 185 kilometers of sandy coastline stretch beautifully. From a distance, the sea of Qinhuangdao seems endless, with white waves merging into the horizon. As you approach the shallow coastline, flocks of seagulls gather on the sandy beach, resembling silhouettes.

湿地海洋风光
Wetland Marine Scenery

海洋大漠风光
Desert Ocean Scenery

海上日出风光
Scenic Sunrise the Sea

海上日落风光
Scenic Sunset the Sea

冬季海冰风光

Scenery of Winter Sea Ice

秦皇岛因山而秀

Qinhuangdao's Beauty Lies in its Mountains

燕山山脉与广阔海疆奇迹般地邂逅，
共同绘就了一幅"长城内外，惟余莽莽"
"暮卷涛声看海浴，朝飞霞翠挹山妍"的
独具魅力的山海壮丽画卷。

The Yanshan Mountain range meets the vast sea in a miraculous convergence, creating a stunning landscape of mountains and seas, like the lines "Within the Great Wall, only endless mountains remain" and "At dusk, watching the sea bath with the sound of waves, at dawn, seeing the colorful mountains bathed in morning light".

碣石山

Mount Jieshi

碣石山
位于昌黎县，
由近百座连绵起伏的峰峦组成，
在数十里范围之内，
岭岭相携，峰峰偎依，
素有"天下神岳""神岳碣石"之美称，
秦始皇、汉武帝、曹操、唐太宗等
帝王在此留下了壮美诗篇。

Mount Jieshi, located in Changli County, consists of nearly a hundred peaks that connect and rise in a sweeping range. This area, known as the "Divine Mountain of the World", and "Sacred Mountain Jieshi", has left its mark on history with emperors like Qin Shi Huang, Emperor Wu of Han, Cao Cao, and Emperor Taizong of Tang, who all left behind majestic poems here.

祖山
Mount Zu

祖山

位于青龙满族自治县，

山势跌宕，峰峦陡峻，

因山势高大、群峰簇拥，

被尊为"群山之祖"，

故称"祖山"。

祖山有奇峰、怪石、云海、秀水、佛光等独特自然风光。

天女木兰花是祖山的稀有花卉，

每年 6 月盛开，

冰清玉洁，超凡脱俗。

Mount Zu situated in Manchu Autonomous County of Qinglong, is renowned for its undulating terrain and steep peaks. Revered as the "Ancestor of All Ranges" , it serves as the geological progenitor for the mountain systems north of the Bohai Sea and east of the Yanshan Mountains, its branching ridges having shaped the region's iconic topography. It features unique natural landscapes such as strange peaks, odd rocks, sea of clouds, beautiful waters, and Mirages. The celestial Mulan flowers, rare to Mount Zu, bloom each June, exuding pure and otherworldly beauty.

角山
Mount Jiao

角山

位于山海关区，

山峰挺拔对峙，

山顶有巨石嵯岈，

恰似龙首戴角，

故而得名"角山"。

角山盘旋于崇山峻岭之上，

是万里长城自山海关向北绵延

所跨越的第一座山峰。

Mount Jiao is located in Shanhaiguan District. The peaks stand tall and face each other, with massive boulders on top resembling a dragon's head adorned with horns, which is why it is named "Mount Jiao" (Horn Mountain). Mount Jiao is the first mountain the Great Wall crosses as it stretches northward from Shanhaiguan.

| 碣石山 |
| Mount Jieshi |

联峰山

Mount Lianfeng

联峰山

位于北戴河海滨风景区西部，

因状似莲蓬，

故又名莲蓬山。

其傍海东西横列 5 公里多，

恰似大海的锦绣屏风。

联峰山山峦俊秀，

林深谷幽，

奇石怪洞，

比比皆是。

Mount Lianfeng, located in the western part of the Beidaihe Seaside Scenic Area, is also known as Lotus Pod Mountain due to its lotus pod-shaped peaks. Stretching over more than five kilometers along the coast, it resembles a magnificent screen protecting the sea. The mountain is known for its beautiful peaks, dense forests, quiet valleys, and numerous strange rocks and caves.

都山
Mount Du

都山
位于青龙满族自治县县城西北部。
这里山奇水秀，群峰陡峻，
云舒雾卷，恍若仙境，
是人们回归自然、返璞归真、
避暑观光、体验满族风情的绝佳之地。

Mount Du, located northwest of Manchu Autonomous County of Qinglong, is known for its spectacular landscapes, with steep peaks and beautiful waters. The mist that wraps around the mountain peaks creates a mystical atmosphere, making it an ideal place for people seeking to return to nature, enjoy summer vacations, and experience the Manchu culture.

秦皇岛因长城而更加雄奇

Qinhuangdao is Majestic with the Great Wall

秦皇岛拥有丰富的长城文化资源。

横亘在市域内 223.1 公里的明长城，

东起山海关老龙头入海石城，

经山海关区、海港区、抚宁区、卢龙县、青龙满族自治县，

西至青龙城子岭口，

是明长城的精华地段。

Qinhuangdao has abundant Great Wall cultural resources. The Great Wall of the Ming Dynasty stretches for 223.1 kilometers across the city, starting from Laolongtou (Old Dragon's Head) where the Great Wall meets the sea, passing through Shanhaiguan District, Haigang District, Funing District, Lulong County, and Manchu Autonomous County of Qinglong, and ending at Qinglong Chengzi Ridge. This stretch of the Great Wall is the most essential part of the Ming Great Wall.

正冠岭
Zhengguanling

董家口
Dongjiakou

界岭口
Jielingkou

城子峪
Chengziyu

秦皇岛因气候而更加怡人

Qinhuangdao is Pleasant for Its Climate

秦皇岛属暖温带半湿润季风型大陆性气候，
冬无严寒，夏无酷暑，
年平均气温 11.3℃，
夏季平均气温 24.2℃，
是著名的避暑胜地。

在秦皇岛观景览胜，

清新的空气沁润着心脾。

被山海环抱的秦皇岛正是因为良好的生态环境，

让人记住了她

春的柔美、夏的热烈、秋的缤纷、冬的深邃。

Qinhuangdao enjoys a warm temperate semi-humid monsoon-influenced continental climate, with mild winters and cool summers. The annual average temperature is 11.3°C, with an average summer temperature of 24.2°C, making it a famous summer retreat. The fresh air in Qinhuangdao refreshes the soul, and the city, embraced by mountains and the sea, is unforgettable for its beautiful spring, vibrant summer, colorful autumn, and profound winter.

生态良好、环境优美是秦皇岛最亮丽的品牌。

饮用水水源地和近岸海域环境功能区水质达标率均为 100%，

重点海水浴场水质达到一类标准。

全市森林覆盖率达到 40.97%，

空气负氧离子含量每立方厘米超过 8000 个，

整座城市犹如一座"天然氧吧"。

The excellent ecology and beautiful environment are Qinhuangdao's most shining features. The water quality of its drinking water sources and nearshore sea areas meet 100% of the standards, and the water quality of key beaches meets Grade A standards. The city's forest coverage rate is 40.97%, and the air has a high concentration of negative oxygen ions, exceeding 8,000 per cubic centimeter, making the entire city a "natural oxygen bar".

秦皇岛湿地总面积 43572.2 公顷，

有 1 处国家级湿地类型自然保护区和

3 处国家级湿地公园，

吸引了 500 余种鸟类在此栖息，

被中国野生动物保护协会授予

"中国观鸟之都"称号。

Qinhuangdao boasts a total wetland area of 43,572.2
hectares, featuring one national wetland nature reserve
and three national wetland parks. These wetlands provide
a habitat for over 500 species of birds, earning the city
the title of "Birdwatching Capital of China" from the
China Wildlife Conservation Association.

| 北戴河国家湿地公园 |
| Beidaihe National Wetland Park |

肆 产业高精尖

战略性新兴产业推动高质量发展

ADVANCED INDUSTRIES
STRATEGIC EMERGING INDUSTRIES DRIVE
HIGH-QUALITY DEVELOPMENT

这就是秦皇岛
THIS IS QINHUANGDAO

步入新时代，

秦皇岛抓住用好京津冀协同发展重大机遇，

进一步全面深化改革，

扩大高水平对外开放，

建设现代产业体系，

加快培育和发展新质生产力。

大力发展生命健康、新型能源、

电子信息、高端装备制造、

生物制造、人工智能、

应用型机器人等特色主导产业，

壮大新兴产业，

培育未来产业，

打造传统产业升级版。

Entering the new era, Qinhuangdao seizes the major opportunity of the coordinated development of the Beijing-Tianjin-Hebei region, further deepening reforms, expanding high-level opening up, and building a modern industrial system. The city accelerates the cultivation and development of new productive forces by focusing on the growth of leading industries such as life and health, new energy, electronic information, high-end equipment manufacturing, biomanufacturing, artificial intelligence, and applied robotics. These efforts aim to strengthen emerging industries, nurture future industries, and upgrade traditional industries.

秦皇岛
拥有秦皇岛港 耀华玻璃 中铁山桥 知名百年企业

Qinhuangdao Hosts Well-Known Centenary Enterprises, Including Qinhuangdao Port, Yaohua Glass, and China Railway Shanhaiguan Bridge

秦皇岛港开埠于 1898 年，
是位于东北、华北咽喉地带的天然不冻良港。
历经百余年岁月洗礼，秦皇岛港蝶变焕新生、奋楫启新程，
实现了向世界级现代化大港的华丽转身。
秦皇岛港口工业旅游区成为
全省首个由港口转型的国家 4A 级旅游景区。
秦皇岛港煤三期码头、煤四期及扩容码头、煤五期码头获评
全国首家"五星级"绿色港区。
作为全国首家获批国家级服务业标准化试点项目的干散货港口企业，
秦皇岛港正着力做好港、产、城和综合交通、开放联动等文章，
不断加快推进智慧、绿色、高效、平安"四型"港口建设，
打造"零废码头"和"花园式港口"，
加快建设国际知名旅游港和现代综合贸易港。

Qinhuangdao Port opened in 1898 and is a natural ice-free harbor located at the strategic throat of Northeast and North China. After more than a century of development, Qinhuangdao Port has undergone a remarkable transformation and is evolving into a world-class modern port. The Qinhuangdao Port Industrial Tourism Zone has become the province's first national 4A-level tourist attraction transformed from a port. The Phase III, Phase IV (including its expansion), and Phase V coal terminals of Qinhuangdao Port have been recognized as the country's first "Five-Star" green port zones, marking the successful transformation of the port. As the first bulk port enterprise in China approved as a national-level service standardization pilot project, Qinhuangdao Port is focusing on integrating port, industry, city, and comprehensive transportation with open cooperation. The port is accelerating the construction of a "smart, green, efficient, and safe" port, aiming to build a "zero-waste terminal" and a "garden-style port". Efforts are underway to transform it into an internationally renowned tourism port and modern integrated trade port.

1922 年，耀华玻璃在秦皇岛成立，

是中国乃至远东第一家采用机器连续制造玻璃的工厂，

奠定了"玻璃之城"的发展基底。

2022 年，新的千亩玻璃产业园拔地而起。

优质浮法玻璃、汽车玻璃生产线

采用脱硫脱硝除尘一体化等国际领先技术，

成为引领玻璃工业转型升级的标杆。

如今，耀华玻璃正续写百年荣光，做优浮法玻璃、

做强加工玻璃、做精特种玻璃，创新特色产品，

将百年耀华打造成为行业一流玻璃材料供应商，

向着"百年耀华、特色耀华、百亿企业"目标迈进。

China Yaohua Glass Group Co., Ltd. was established in Qinhuangdao in 1922, and was the first glass factory in China and even the Far East to use continuous machine manufacturing. This laid the foundation for the development of the "Glass City". In 2022, a new glass industrial park covering thousands of acres was established, using international leading technologies such as desulfurization, denitrification, and dust removal in its float glass and automotive glass production lines. Yaohua Glass is now continuing its century-long legacy of excellence. By refining float glass, strengthening processed glass, perfecting specialty glass, and innovating unique products, it is transforming itself into a top-tier glass material supplier in the industry. Yaohua is advancing toward its ambitious goals of becoming a "Century-Old Yaohua, a Distinctive Yaohua, and a Ten-Billion-Yuan Enterprise".

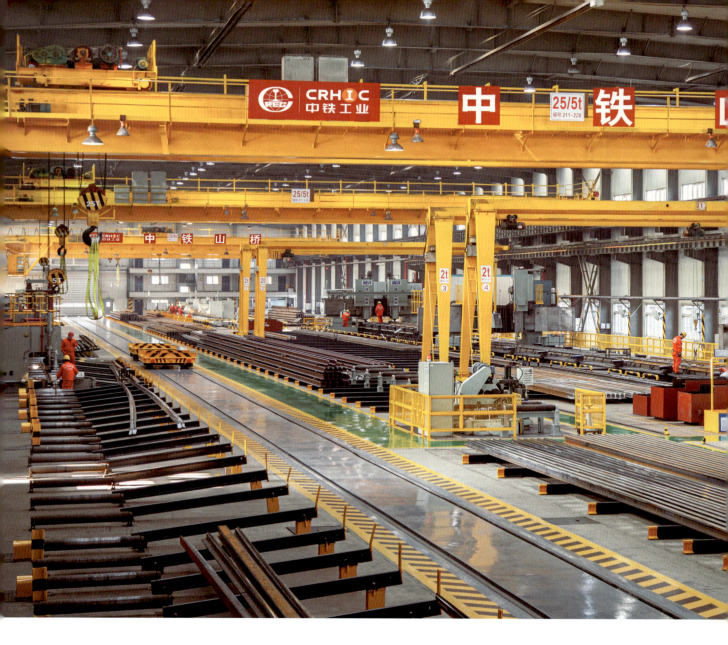

中铁山桥始建于 1894 年，
前身是中国第一家铁路钢桥制造厂
——北洋官铁路局山海关造桥厂，
是我国生产桥梁钢结构和
铁路道岔等产品建厂最早、
行业领先、技术一流的制造企业，
已累计制造各类钢桥 3200 余座、
铁路道岔 40 余万组，
被誉为"中国钢桥的摇篮、道岔的故乡"。

从武汉长江大桥、
南京长江大桥到港珠澳大桥、
孟加拉国帕德玛大桥，
从时速 35 公里普通铁路道岔到时速 350 公里高速铁路道岔，
一次又一次刷新着中国跨度与中国速度，
为中国桥梁、中国高铁两张国家名片融入了重要的山桥元素。

China Railway Shanhaiguan Bridge Group Co., Ltd. , established in 1894, originated as Shanhaiguan Bridge Factory under the Beiyang Government Railway Bureau—China's first railway steel bridge manufacturing plant. It is the earliest and leading enterprise in China's steel bridge and railway turnout industry, renowned for its cutting-edge technology. To date, it has produced over 3,200 steel bridges and 400,000 sets of railway turnouts, earning titles such as the "Cradle of Steel Bridges" and "Hometown of Railway Turnouts" in China. From iconic bridges like the Wuhan Yangtze River Bridge and Nanjing Yangtze River Bridge to modern marvels such as the Hong Kong-Zhuhai-Macao Bridge and Bangladesh's Padma Bridge, and from 35 km/h conventional railway turnouts to 350 km/h high-speed railway turnouts, China Railway Shanhaiguan Bridge Group has continuously redefined China's engineering span and speed, infusing critical elements of its expertise into the nation's iconic achievements in bridge engineering and high-speed rail.

秦皇岛
拥有国家级北戴河生命健康产业创新示范区

Qinhuangdao Has a National-Level Health and Life Sciences Industry Innovation Demonstration Zone in Beidaihe

2016 年，国务院批准设立北戴河生命健康产业创新示范区。
2023 年 2 月，国家发展改革委等 9 部委出台了
支持北戴河生命健康产业创新示范区发展"7+6"政策，
为秦皇岛跑赢生命健康产业新赛道注入了新的活力和动力。
秦皇岛以国家"7+6"支持政策出台为契机，
锚定中国康养名城目标，
打造医、药、养、健、游"五位一体"、
"健康服务业、健康制造业双轮驱动"新格局。

In 2016, the State Council approved the establishment of the Beidaihe Life and Health Industry Innovation Demonstration Zone. In February 2023, the National Development and Reform Commission and nine other ministries issued a set of "7+6" policies to foster the development of this zone, injecting new vitality and momentum into Qinhuangdao's race in the life and health industry. Seizing the opportunity presented by the national "7+6" support policies, Qinhuangdao has set its sights on becoming a leading health and wellness city in China. It is working to create a new pattern of development driven by both the "five-in-one" integration of medicine, pharmaceuticals, wellness, fitness, and tourism, as well as the "dual engine" development of health services and health manufacturing.

在创新示范区内，
生命健康产业集聚成势。
以发展生物制造产业为重点，
依托河北省合成生物制造技术创新中心
及成果转化基地，
聚焦生物能源、生物材料、生物医药
三大方向布局合成生物制造赛道，
打造合成生物技术全产业链条。
全球首个生物合成胆红素已成功生产，
生物制造产业走在了全国前列。

Within the Innovation Demonstration Zone, the life and health industry is rapidly developing. The focus is on the development of the biomanufacturing industry, with the support of the Hebei Academy of Sciences Synthetic Biology Manufacturing Technology Innovation Center and its technology commercialization base. The area is concentrating on three key areas: bioenergy, biomaterials, and biomedicine. It aims to create a complete industrial chain for synthetic biology, and the world's first biosynthetic bilirubin has already been successfully produced, positioning Qinhuangdao at the forefront of the biomanufacturing industry in China.

康泰医学

是一家专业从事医疗仪器研发生产、

提供远程医疗和健康管理的公司。

作为国内最大的医疗仪器研发生产基地之一，

康泰医学年生产各类医疗器械 100 万台（套），

产品销至全球 130 多个国家和地区，

"物联网健康一体机"项目被列入

国家火炬计划产业化示范项目，

"康泰"已成为医疗器械行业中最知名的品牌之一。

Contec Medical Systems Co., Ltd. is a company specializing in the research and development of medical devices, offering telemedicine and health management services. As one of the largest R&D and production bases for medical instruments in China, it manufactures 1 million medical devices annually, exporting its products to over 130 countries and regions worldwide. The company's "Internet of Things Health Integration Machine" project has been included in the national Torch Program for industrialization demonstration. Contec has become one of the most well-known brands in the medical device industry.

华恒生物

是国家绿色工厂、

国家专精特新"小巨人"、

国家知识产权优势企业，

主要产品包括 L-丙氨酸、DL-丙氨酸、

β-丙氨酸、苹果酸等生物基产品。

"人工智能设计生物酶蛋白高效制造 β-丙氨酸成果转化"

被列为河北省重大成果转化项目。

2023 年，企业投建 5 万吨生物基 L-苹果酸项目，

正着力打造全球最大的绿色有机苹果酸智能化生产基地。

Qinhuangdao Huaheng Biotechnology Co., Ltd. is a national-level green factory, a national "specialized and innovative small giant", and a leading company in intellectual property in China. Its main products include L-alanine, DL-alanine, β-alanine, malic acid, and other bio-based products. The company's project on the "AI-Designed Biological Enzyme Protein Efficient Manufacturing of β-Alanine" has been recognized as a key project for technology transformation in Hebei Province. In 2023, the company launched a 50,000-ton bio-based L-malic acid project, working towards establishing the world's largest green organic malic acid intelligent production base.

这就是秦皇岛

1-60

秦皇岛
是汽车零部件制造基地

Qinhuangdao is an Automobile Parts Manufacturing Base

拥有中信戴卡、威卡威、艾杰旭等领军企业，

形成了以汽车轮毂、内外饰件、玻璃、管路、轿车门等为主导的产品结构，

建成了世界最大的铝车轮和铝制汽车底盘零部件生产加工基地，

轮毂制造水平居全球首位。

Qinhuangdao is home to leading enterprises such as CITIC Dicastal, WKW, and AGC. The city has developed a product structure dominated by automotive wheels, interior/exterior trims, glass, pipes, and car doors, establishing the world's largest production and processing base for aluminum wheels and aluminum automotive chassis components. It ranks first globally in wheel manufacturing.

续发展
le Development

★ 中国压铸件生产企业综合实力50强
Top 50 Die Casting Manufacturers in China by General Strength
★ 铃轩奖量产类·底盘类优秀奖
Lingxuan Award for Excellence in Mass Production - Chassis Category
★ 中国人才发展菁英奖·最佳学习项目奖
China Talent Development Award - The Best Learning Project Award

中信戴卡

2021 年被评为世界"灯塔工厂",

成为全球汽车铝制零部件行业的

首个"灯塔工厂"。

2025 年,

该企业摩洛哥生产基地入选"灯塔工厂",

成为非洲第一家"灯塔工厂"。

该企业的装备和智能制造能力达到了全球同行业最高水平,

获评国家级大数据产业发展示范和国家级工业互联网试点示范。

企业生产的铝制汽车轮毂连续十多年蝉联全球销量冠军,

占全球市场规模的 1/3,

全球每三辆汽车中就有一辆使用中信戴卡的产品。

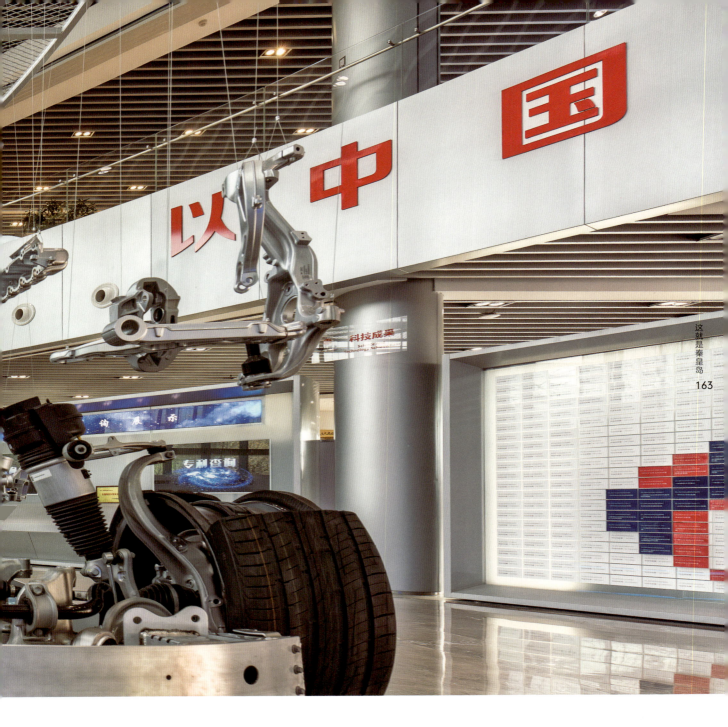

In 2021, CITIC Dicastal Co., Ltd. was recognized as a "Lighthouse Factory" by the World Economic Forum, becoming the first in the global automotive aluminum parts industry to earn this title. In 2025, its Moroccan production base was also selected as a "Lighthouse Factory", becoming the first in Africa. The company's equipment and smart manufacturing capabilities have reached the highest global standards, earning recognition as a national-level big data industry development model and a national-level industrial internet pilot demonstration. CITIC Dicastal has maintained its position as the global sales leader for aluminum wheels for over ten years, accounting for one-third of the global market, with one in every three cars in the world using its products.

威卡威

作为乘用车内外饰件系统的综合性制造商与服务商，

具备强大的自动化、智能化的产品模块生产能力，

同步开发、整体配套方案设计能力，

以及可视化、数字化管理能力。

企业在中国中高档乘用车内外饰行业中处于领先地位，

拉弯、冲压和氧化等工艺技术达到全球先进水平。

Qinhuangdao WKW Automotive Parts Co., Ltd., as a comprehensive manufacturer and service provider of passenger car interior and exterior trim systems, possesses strong capabilities in automated and intelligent product module production, synchronized development, overall solution design, and visualization and digital management. The company leads the domestic market for mid-to-high-end passenger car interior and exterior trim, with global-leading standards in processes such as bending, stamping, and oxidation.

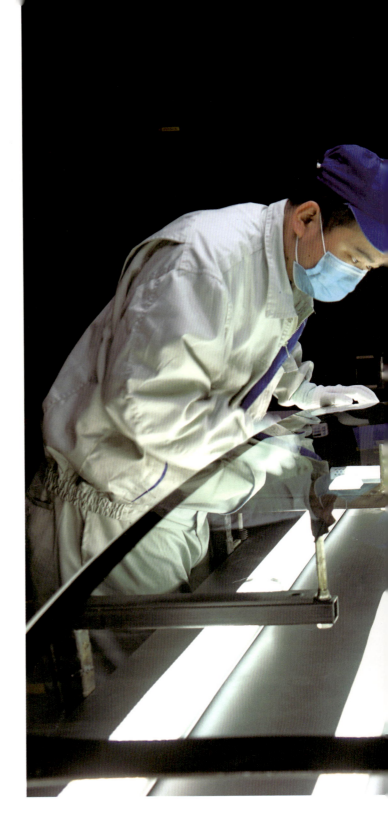

艾杰旭

是中国第二大汽车玻璃生产基地，
拥有制造全系列汽车安全玻璃、
能代表世界领先水平的技术和生产设备，
为丰田、本田、日产、大众、宝马、奔驰、
沃尔沃、现代、标致、铃木、五十铃等
国际知名汽车公司提供配套服务。

AGC Automotive (Qinhuangdao) Co., Ltd. is China's
second-largest automotive glass production base,
with the capability to manufacture a full range of
automotive safety glass using world-leading technology
and production equipment. It provides services to
internationally renowned automobile manufacturers
such as Toyota, Honda, Nissan, Volkswagen, BMW,
Mercedes-Benz, Volvo, Hyundai, Peugeot, Suzuki, and
Isuzu.

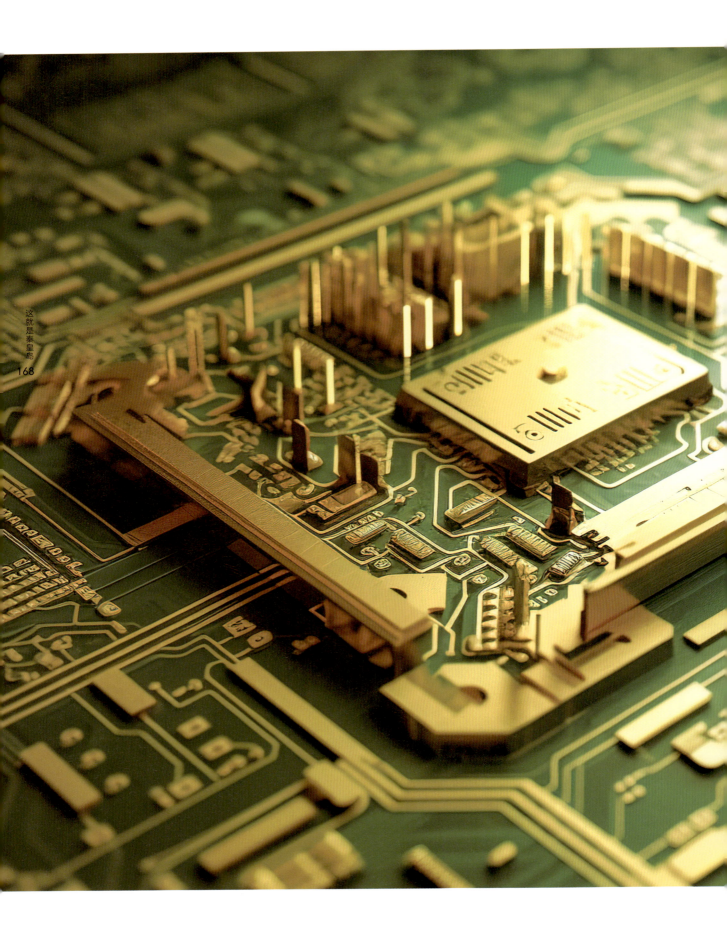

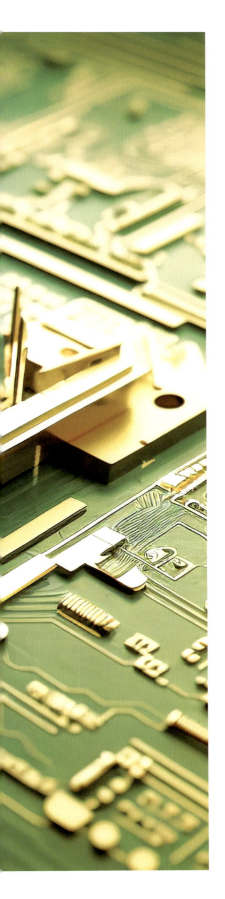

秦皇岛
是印制电路板生产基地

Qinhuangdao is a Printed Circuit Board Manufacturing Base

秦皇岛电子信息产业发展迅速，

主要集中在电子元器件、消防电子、医疗电子等领域，

培育出宏启胜、海湾公司、泰和安等一批优质企业。

Qinhuangdao's electronic information manufacturing industry is developing rapidly, focusing on areas such as electronic components, fire safety electronics, and medical electronics. The city has nurtured high-quality enterprises such as Hongqisheng, Gulf Security Technology, and Tanda.

臻鼎科技集团

于 2007 年开始在秦皇岛投资，

先后设立了宏启胜精密电子（秦皇岛）有限公司、

礼鼎半导体科技秦皇岛有限公司。

2017 年投资了具有国际领先技术水平的

高阶高密度印制电路板项目，

打造以工业 4.0 为目标的智能工厂，

树立了业界标杆。

2021 年投资高端集成电路封装载板智能制造项目，

弥补了国内集成电路半导体芯片封装载板技术短板，

大大提高了半导体芯片载板自给率。

Zhending Technology Group began investing in Qinhuangdao in 2007 and has established Hongqisheng Precision Electronics (Qinhuangdao) Co., Ltd. and Liding Semiconductor Technology Qinhuangdao Co., Ltd. In 2017, it invested in an internationally leading high-end high-density printed circuit board project and built an intelligent factory targeting Industry 4.0, setting an industry benchmark. In 2021, it invested in a high-end integrated circuit packaging board intelligent manufacturing project, addressing the domestic shortfall in integrated circuit semiconductor chip packaging board technology and significantly increasing the self-sufficiency rate of semiconductor chip packaging boards.

海湾公司

是国内主要的火灾探测报警

及消防整体解决方案供应商之一。

自 1993 年成立以来，

海湾已成为中国消防行业的主要品牌，

广受用户认可。

秦皇岛消防电子产业

产能占全国消防电子行业的 40% 左右，

每年全球大约有 50 万个房间安装了

秦皇岛生产的消防电子感烟探测器，

"Made in QHD" 已经成为消防电子领域的

一张亮丽名片。

Gulf Security Technology Co., Ltd is one of the main suppliers of fire detection, alarm, and integrated fire protection solutions in China. Since its establishment in 1993, it has become a leading brand in China's fire safety industry, widely recognized by users. Qinhuangdao's fire electronics sector accounts for approximately 40% of the nation's total production capacity. Every year, approximately 500,000 rooms worldwide are equipped with fire electronic smoke detectors produced in Qinhuangdao. "Made in QHD" has become a shining label in the fire safety electronics field.

秦皇岛
是重型装备出海口基地 百万吨造船基地
Qinhuangdao is a Heavy Equipment Export Base and a Million-Ton Shipbuilding Base

秦皇岛高端装备制造业主要集中在船舶与海洋工程装备、能源装备、电力装备以及环保、冶金等专用机械制造领域，形成了以山船重工、哈电重装、天威秦变、中油宝世顺等企业为龙头的高端装备制造业产业集群。

The high-end equipment manufacturing industry in Qinhuangdao is mainly concentrated in sectors such as shipbuilding and offshore engineering equipment, energy equipment, power equipment, and specialized machinery manufacturing for environmental protection and metallurgy. The city has formed a high-end equipment manufacturing industrial cluster, led by companies such as Shanhaiguan Shipbuilding Industry Co., Ltd., Harbin Electric Group (Qinhuangdao) Heavy Equipment Co., Ltd., Tianwei Qinbian Electric Co., Ltd, and Zhongyou Baoshishun (Qinhuangdao) Pipe Co., Ltd.

山船重工
是北方重要的修造船企业之一，
具备年造船 160 万载重吨、
年修船 300 艘的生产能力。
产品涵盖集装箱船、散货船、油轮三种市场主力船型。
成功建造世界首艘海洋风车安装船，
完成世界首艘单壳油船改装为双层矿砂船、
国内船厂首个 FPSO 改装工程等，
建造的全省最大吨位原油轮已交付使用，
填补了河北省中大型油轮的空白。

Shanhaiguan Shipbuilding Industry Co., Ltd. is one of the important shipbuilding companies in Northern China, with an annual shipbuilding capacity of 1.6 million tons and the ability to repair 300 ships per year. The company's products include three main types of ships: container ships, bulk carriers, and oil tankers. It successfully built the world's first offshore wind turbine installation vessel and completed the world's first conversion of a single-hull oil tanker to a double-hull bulk carrier. The company also delivered the largest oil tanker in the province, filling the gap for medium and large oil tankers in Hebei.

这就是华龙

哈电重装

生产的"华龙一号"蒸汽发生器实现了
我国第三代核电设备制造自主可控，
技术达到了世界领先水平。
该企业已经掌握多种技术路线
核电设备制造技术，
每年可生产6台（套）核电核岛主设备，
实现了蒸汽发生器批量化制造。

Harbin Electric Group (Qinhuangdao) Heavy
Equipment Co., Ltd.'s production of the "Hualong
One" HL-T67 steam generator has positioned
China at the forefront of third-generation nuclear
power technology. The company can produce six
sets of nuclear island main equipment annually.
It has mastered multiple technical routes and
manufacturing technologies for nuclear power
equipment and has achieved mass production of
steam generators.

这就是秦皇岛

哈电通用

生产的首台国产 HA 级重型燃气轮机于 2023 年 2 月顺利下线。

该重型燃气轮机代表着全球最顶尖的制造水平，

被称为"工业皇冠上的明珠"。

它的下线标志着中国重型燃气轮机生产制造水平实现新突破，

使秦皇岛成为通用电气全球三大燃机制造基地之一。

Harbin Electric General's first domestically produced HA-class heavy-duty gas turbine was successfully rolled off the production line In February 2023. This technology represents the world's highest level, known as the "pearl on the crown of industry". Its manufacture marks a new breakthrough in China's heavy-duty gas turbine production, making Qinhuangdao one of GE's three global gas turbine manufacturing bases.

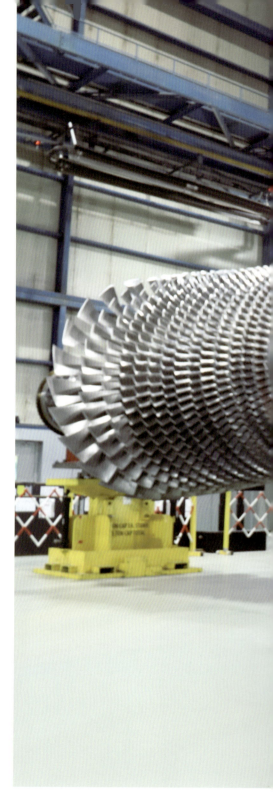

天威秦变

是国家电网、南方电网、三峡集团、

中核集团、中广核及五大发电集团的

主要供应商，

为乌东德、白鹤滩水电站，秦山核电站，

皖电东送工程、

吉泉直流工程、

青豫直流工程等

提供了大量高端变压器产品。

Tianwei Qinbian Electric Co., Ltd is a major supplier to the State Grid, China Southern Power Grid, China Three Gorges Corporation, China National Nuclear Corporation, China General Nuclear Power Group, and the five major power generation groups. The company has provided advanced transformer products for landmark projects such as the Wudongde and Baihetan hydropower stations, Qinshan Nuclear Power Plant, the East Anhui Power Transmission Project, the Jiquan UHVDC Transmission Project, and the Qingyu UHVDC Transmission Project.

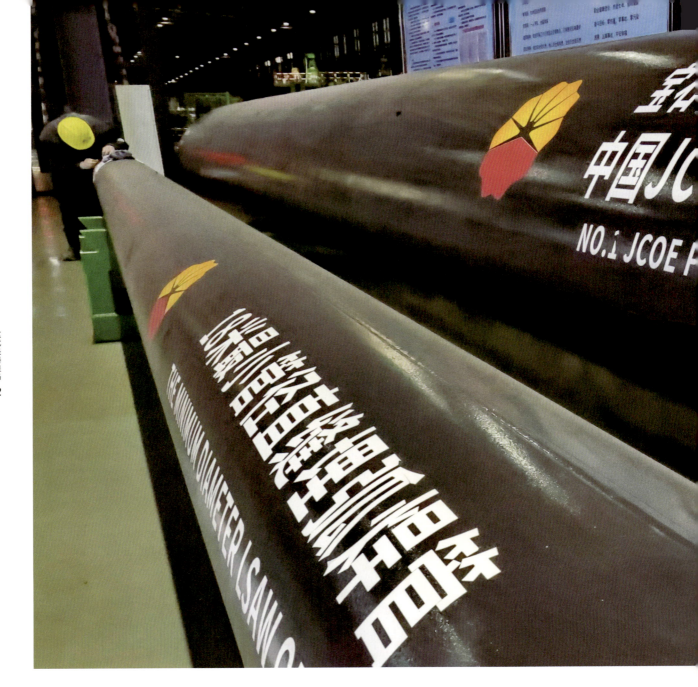

中油宝世顺

已建成世界首条螺旋、

直缝双工艺焊管生产线，

产品出口到亚洲、非洲、欧洲、美洲等的

20 多个国家和地区，

为西气东输、中俄东线、蒙西天然气、陕京线等

国内几乎所有的重大管线提供优质钢管 400 余万吨，

成为国家管网、中石油、中石化、中海油等集团的主力供应商。

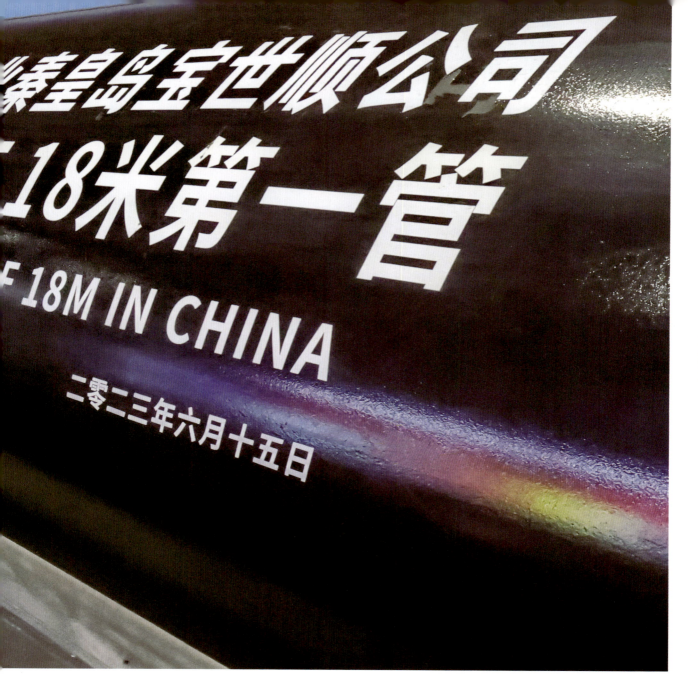

Zhongyou Baoshishun (Qinhuangdao) Pipe Co., Ltd. has established the world's first spiral and straight seam dual-process welded pipe production line. Its products are exported to over 20 countries and regions across Asia, Africa, Europe, and America, supplying over 4 million tons of high-quality steel pipes for major domestic pipelines such as the West-to-East Gas Transmission Project, the China-Russia East Line, the Mongolia-Western China natural gas pipeline, and the Shaanxi-Beijing pipeline. It has become a key supplier for groups including the national pipeline network, China National Petroleum Corporation, Sinopec, and China National Offshore Oil Corporation.

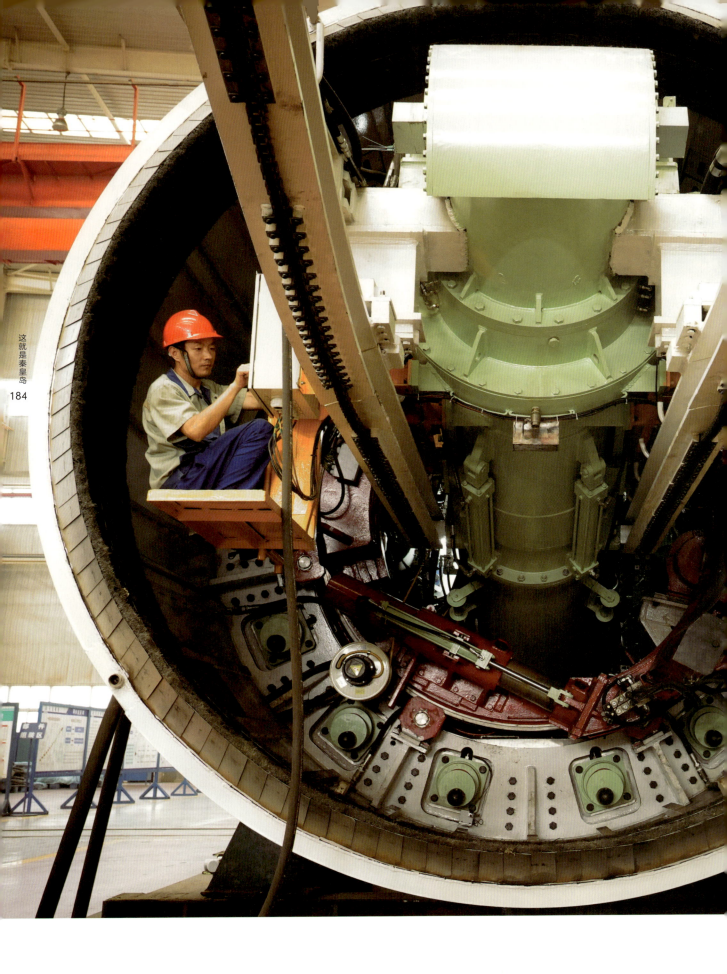

天业通联

是国内顶级铁路桥梁施工起重运输设备供应商，

自主研发了世界最大吨位 1100 吨运架一体式架桥机，

整体技术达到了世界领先水平。

Qinhuangdao Tianye Tolian Heavy Industry&Technology Co., Ltd is a top domestic supplier of railway bridge construction, lifting, and transport equipment. It has self-developed 1,100-ton bridge-launching crane, the largest in the world, representing the cutting edge of global technology.

| 1100 吨运架一体式架桥机 |
| 1100-ton Bridge Girder Erection Machine with Integrated Transport Function |

秦皇岛
是玻璃及铝制品生产加工基地

Qinhuangdao is a Glass and Aluminum Products Manufacturing Base

秦皇岛在先进金属材料、新型功能材料、

高性能纤维及复合材料等领域，

具有较强的技术和市场优势。

Qinhuangdao has strong technical and market advantages in the fields of advanced metal materials, new functional materials, high-performance fibers, and composite materials.

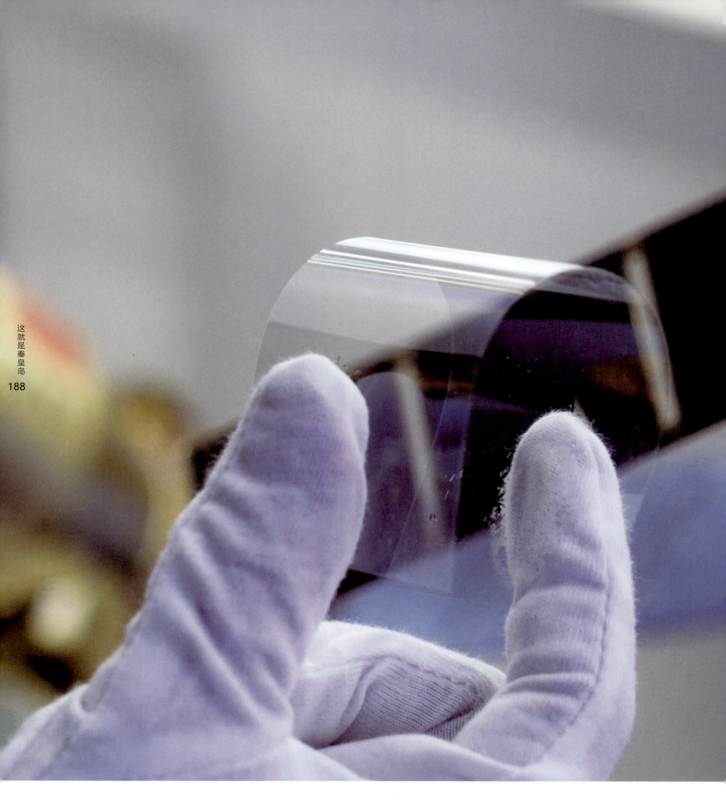

星箭特种玻璃
研发生产的产品主要应用于系列载人飞船及
探测卫星等航天领域。
该系列产品能有效抵挡太空中高能粒子
对太阳能电池板的冲击，
堪称航天器的"护身金甲"。
公司研发的 0.01 毫米超薄耐高温光学玻璃，
薄如蝉翼，却坚如铠甲，
耐得住瞬间 1200℃ 高温，
是我国光学玻璃领域的一项重大突破。
2000 年至今，
我国发射的卫星和飞船都有星箭玻璃保驾护航。

Xingjian Special Glass develops and produces products mainly used in crewed spacecraft and exploratory satellites, effectively protecting solar panels from the impact of high-energy particles in space. This series of products can be considered the "armor" of spacecraft. The company also developed 0.01mm ultra-thin, high-temperature-resistant optical glass, which is thinner as a cicada's wing but as strong as armor, able to withstand sudden temperatures of 1200℃. This product marks a significant breakthrough in China's optical glass sector. Since 2000, all the satellites and spacecraft launched by China have been protected by Xingjian glass.

奥科宁克
拥有两条大扁锭生产线、
先进的全套 1+3 热连轧机组、
VAI 冷轧机和相关精整设备，
主要生产铝金属包装产品、
交通运输用铝材、
汽车轻量化用铝产品、
船舶用铝板及工业用铝材等高端铝板带产品，
是国内铝金属包装材料重点供应商。

Arconic (Qinhuangdao) Aluminum Industries Co., Ltd. has two large billet production lines, advanced 1+3 hot-rolling mill sets, VAI cold-rolling mills, and related finishing equipment. It mainly produces high-end aluminum plate and strip products such as aluminum metal packaging materials, aluminum for transportation, lightweight aluminum for automobiles, aluminum plates for ships, and industrial aluminum materials, and is a key supplier of aluminum packaging materials in China.

秦皇岛
是粮油食品加工基地

Qinhuangdao

is a Grain and Oil Food Processing Base

粮油食品加工是秦皇岛传统优势产业。

秦皇岛拥有金海食品、金海粮油、正大食品等

一批粮油食品加工龙头骨干企业，

建设千亿级粮油食品加工基地未来可期。

Grain and oil food processing is a traditional advantageous industry in Qinhuangdao, with leading Grain and Oil Food Processing enterprises such as Qinhuangdao Goldensea Foodstuff Industries Co., Ltd. and Charoen Pokphand Foods. The city is expected to build a trillion-level grain and oil food processing base in the future.

金海食品

是目前亚洲生产规模最大、

产业链条延伸最长的大豆蛋白综合生产企业，

产品远销全球 70 多个国家和地区，

正在加快建设益海嘉里（秦皇岛）

粮油食品综合加工园区。

Qinhuangdao Goldensea Foodstuff Industries Co., Ltd. is currently the largest and most extensive soy protein production enterprise in Asia, with a product chain that extends the longest. Its products are exported to over 70 countries and regions around the world. The company is accelerating the construction of the Yihaijiali (Qinhuangdao) grain and oil food processing park.

中储粮海港粮食储备基地项目

是落实国家保粮食能源安全的重点建设项目，

共建造 90 座筒仓，

总储存量可达 83 万吨，

旨在打造"前港中仓后厂"无缝衔接的粮食转运储备及加工体系，

进一步延伸粮油加工产业链条，

有效打通粮食储备和加工上下游环节。

The Sinograin Haigang Grain Reserve Base project is a key national initiative for ensuring food and energy security. It involves the construction of 90 silos with a total storage capacity of up to 830,000 tons. The project aims to build a seamless connection between the port, storage, and processing facilities, further extending the grain and oil processing industry chain and effectively linking the upstream and downstream of grain storage and processing.

秦皇岛
是光伏装备
及核裂变能装备制造基地

Qinhuangdao is a manufacturing base for photovoltaic and nuclear fission energy equipment

秦皇岛陆域和海上风光资源丰富，
拥有风电、光伏发电项目 126 个，
总装机容量可达 1360 万千瓦，
初步形成了"风、光、水、火、核、储、氢"
多能互补的新型能源发展格局，
光伏装备及核裂变能装备生产位居全国前列。

With abundant onshore and offshore wind and solar resources, Qinhuangdao has developed 126 wind and photovoltaic power projects, boasting a total installed capacity of up to 13.6 million kilowatts. The city has initially established a diversified energy development framework that integrates wind, solar, hydro, thermal, nuclear, energy storage, and hydrogen energy. Its production of photovoltaic and nuclear fission energy equipment ranks among the top in the nation.

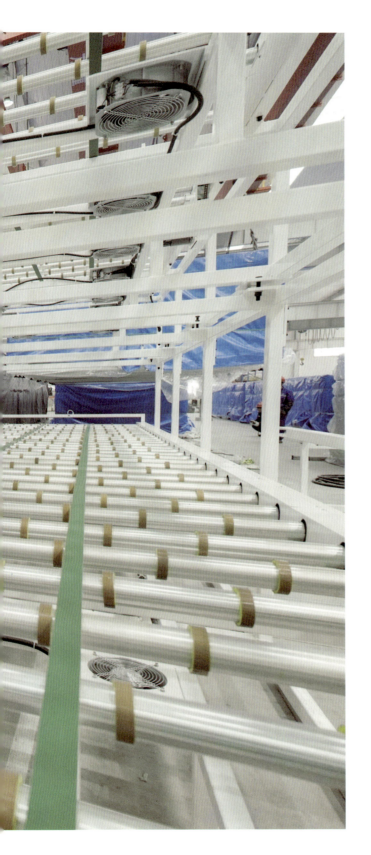

秦皇岛大力推进光伏产业全产业链发展，

汇集了晟成光伏、羿珩科技、

博硕光电、硕谷光伏等

一批光伏层压机重点企业，

形成了"以层压机为龙头，

以光伏基础零部件与关键基础材料为两翼"的

光伏装备产业体系。

全国光伏层压机设备 80% 以上为秦皇岛制造。

Qinhuangdao is vigorously promoting the full industrial chain development of the photovoltaic industry. It has gathered key enterprises such as Qinhuangdao SC-Solar Technology Co., Ltd., Hebei Yiheng Solar Science & Technology Co., Ltd., Qinhuangdao Boostsolar Photovoltaic Equipment Co., Ltd. (Boostsolar), and Qinhuangdao Shuogu Photovoltaic Technology Co., Ltd., forming a photovoltaic equipment industrial system with "laminators as the leading role and photovoltaic basic components and key materials as the two wings". More than 80% of photovoltaic laminating equipment in China is manufactured in Qinhuangdao.

兼具动与静

探索海滨城市生活新模式

HARMONY OF ACTIVITY AND SERENITY
EXPLORING NEW LIFESTYLES IN A COASTAL CITY

这就是秦皇岛
THIS IS QINHUANGDAO

秦皇岛把文体旅游

作为主导产业融合发展，

做"热"文化、

做"活"赛事、

做"火"旅游，

致力于打造宜居宜业宜游的

海滨城市生活新模式。

在这里，

总有一片海、一处景、

一项赛事、一场演出，

能满足你对美好生活的向往。

Qinhuangdao is integrating culture, sports, and tourism as leading industries. It aims to "heat up" culture, "energize" events, and "ignite" tourism, striving to create a new model of seaside city life that is livable, business-friendly, and tourist-friendly. Here, there is always a sea, a scene, an event, or a performance that will fulfill your yearning for a beautiful life.

这里是文艺青年的心灵港湾

Here is the Spiritual Haven for Young Artists

新型旅游社区阿那亚
入选《时代周刊》评选的
"2024 年全球 100 个最佳旅行目的地"，
是无数文艺青年心中的网红艺术打卡地，
孤独图书馆、海边礼堂、沙丘美术馆等建筑
独具文艺范儿。

The new tourism community, Aranya, was listed by Time Magazine as one of the "Top 100 Best Travel Destinations in 2024". It is a popular artistic hub for young artists, with unique architectural landmarks such as the Lonely Library, the Seaside Chapel, and the Dune Art Gallery, all exuding artistic charm.

阿那亚戏剧节

是国内首个海边戏剧节，

每年 6、7 月举办，

活动内容丰富多样，

包括戏剧演出、青年导演峰会、

环境戏剧朗读等系列活动，

成功吸引数百位中外戏剧艺术家参与。

The Aranya Drama Festival is China's first seaside drama festival, held annually in June and July. It includes a series of events such as drama performances, a summit for young directors, and environmental theatre readings, attracting hundreds of domestic and international drama artists.

虾米音乐节

已经在秦皇岛阿那亚连续举办 3 届，

演出场地就在大海边、沙滩上，

动人的音乐、深邃的大海、细软的沙滩，

营造了专属于乐迷的理想之境。

The Xiami Music&Art Festival has been held
consecutively three times at Aranya in Qinhuangdao,
with performances taking place right by the sea
and on the sandy beaches. The enchanting music,
vast ocean, and soft sands create an ideal paradise
exclusively for music enthusiasts.

海浪电影周

每年在秦皇岛阿那亚举办，

是促进华语商业类型片创作、

面向影院观众、

发现青年电影人的电影计划。

观众可以坐在沙滩躺椅上，

吹着习习海风，

欣赏着荧幕电影，

别有一番风味。

Aranya Waves Film Festival is held annually at Aranya in Qinhuangdao. It is a film initiative aimed at promoting the creation of Chinese commercial genre films, targeting cinema audiences, and discovering young filmmakers. Audiences can sit on beach loungers, feel the sea breeze, and watch films on the big screen, offering a unique viewing experience.

大型室内史诗演出《长城》

位于山海关长城脚下，

借助于程控式多轨威亚、

天候模拟系统、

复合式多重影像系统等先进舞台科技手段，

生动重现蒙恬北驱匈奴、

孟姜女哭长城、

秦始皇一统江山等场景。

The large-scale indoor epic performance "Great Wall" is located at the foot of the Shanhaiguan Great Wall. Utilizing advanced stage technologies such as computer-controlled multi-track wire systems, weather simulation systems, and composite multi-image systems, it recreates historical scenes like Meng Tian driving away the Xiongnu to the north, Meng Jiangnu weeping over the Great Wall, and Qin Shi Huang unifying the empire.

長城

中华山海关

GREAT WALL

江山永固　長城不老
山海史传　長城傳奇

大型海上实景演出《浪淘沙·北戴河》

位于北戴河碧螺塔海上酒吧公园。

该演出以毛泽东主席的著名诗词《浪淘沙·北戴河》为主线，

精彩演绎北戴河的前世今生及其所蕴含的浪漫情怀。

The large-scale maritime live performance "Lang Tao Sha : Beidaihe" is situated at the Biluota Bar Park in Beidaihe. Based on Chairman Mao's famous poem "Lang Tao Sha: Beidaihe", it portrays the past and present of Beidaihe along with its romantic sentiments.

这里是中外游客的旅游乐园

A Paradise for Domestic and International Tourists

优质的旅游资源、厚重的文化底蕴

和良好的生态环境，

赋予了大美秦皇岛无尽的魅力，

唱响了"秦皇山海·四季皆游"的旅游品牌，

使秦皇岛成为广大游客心中的诗与远方。

这么近，那么美，周末到河北——秦皇岛等你来！

With high-quality tourism resources, a rich cultural heritage, and a favorable ecological environment, the beautiful Qinhuangdao possesses endless charm. It has become a tourism brand symbolized by "Qinhuang Mountain and Sea, Four Seasons for Travel", drawing visitors who consider Qinhuangdao a place of poetry and distant dreams. So close, so beautiful—weekends in Hebei await you in Qinhuangdao!

蓝色海岸 · 休闲度假游
Blue Coast • Leisure and Vacation Travel

古色长城 · 雄关览胜游
Ancient Great Wall • Majestic Pass Touring

绿色生态 · 康养健身游

Green Ecology • Health and Fitness Tourism

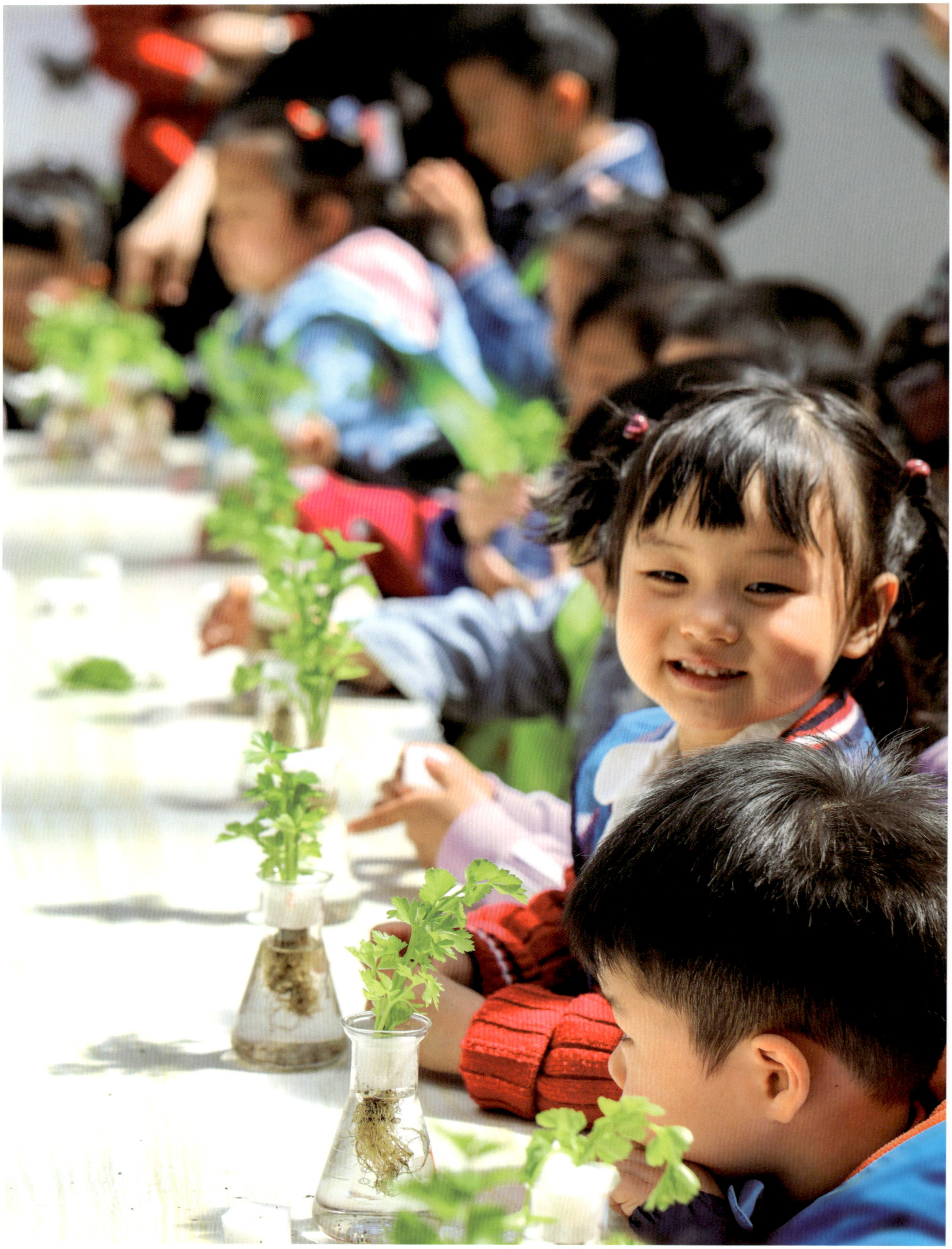

金色青春 · 研学逐梦游
Golden Youth • Study and Travel

红色浪漫·红酒品鉴游
Red Romance • Wine Tasting Tour

这里是运动健将的竞技赛场

A Competitive Arena for Sports Champions

秦皇岛

是全国唯一既协办过亚运会

又协办过奥运会的地级市，

这一殊荣彰显了其独特的地位和影响力。

秦皇岛拥有一批高质量的"国字号"体育设施，

包括国家体育总局秦皇岛训练基地（中国足球学校）、

秦皇岛国家游泳跳水训练基地等。

Qinhuangdao is the only prefecture-level city in the country that has co-hosted both the Asian Games and the Olympic Games, a distinction that highlights its unique position and influence. Qinhuangdao is home to a range of high-quality national sports facilities, including General Administration of Sports Training Base in Qinhuangdao (the China Football School), the Qinhuangdao National Swimming and Diving Training Base.

1990 年北京亚运会，
秦皇岛作为协办城市
成功协办了海上项目帆船帆板竞赛。
2008 年北京奥运会，
秦皇岛作为协办城市
成功协办了 12 场足球比赛。

During the 1990 Beijing Asian Games, Qinhuangdao co-hosted sailing and windsurfing competitions as a co-host city. In the 2008 Beijing Olympic Games, it co-hosted 12 football matches as a co-host city.

秦皇岛马拉松赛自 2014 年开始,

每年 5 月举办,

已成功举办 8 届,

被中国田径协会认定为 A1 类金牌赛事,

是秦皇岛重点打造的国际品牌赛事之一。

The Qinhuangdao Marathon has successfully been held eight times since its inception in 2014. Held annually in May, it has been recognized by the Chinese Athletics Association as a Class A1 Gold Medal event, making it one of Qinhuangdao's key international brand events.

"秦皇岛帆船季"已连续举办 4 季。
每年从 4 月持续至 10 月，
涵盖了从专业级别的全国帆船锦标赛、
全国青年帆船冠军赛，
到面向大众的家庭帆船赛，

是目前国内持续时间最长、
参与人数最多的帆船活动盛会。
北戴河新区蔚蓝海岸和秦皇岛国际旅游港
被评为"中国十大帆船帆板运动目的地"。

The "Qinhuangdao Sailing Season" has been held for four consecutive seasons. Each year from April to October, it encompasses events from the national professional sailing championships and national youth sailing champion races to family sailing competitions for the general public. It is currently the longest-running and most participatory sailing event in the country. Seatopia in the Beidaihe New Area and Qinhuangdao International Tourism Port have been recognized as two of China's "Top Ten Sailing and Windsurfing Destinations".

| 加雷斯 · 大卫 · 波茨 |
| Gareth David Potts |

中式台球大师赛起源于秦皇岛，

已推广至全球 68 个国家和地区，

拥有 8000 余万名爱好者，

被中宣部评为"中华文化走出去"项目。

The Heyball Masters Grand originated in Qinhuangdao and has been promoted to 68 countries and regions worldwide. With over 80 million enthusiasts, it has been designated by the Publicity Department of the Communist Party of China as a "Chinese Culture Going Global" project.

北戴河轮滑节

自 2005 年起已连续举办 20 届，

已成为世界上规模最大的轮滑节庆活动之一。

北戴河先后被国际轮滑联合会、中国轮滑协会

评为"世界轮滑之都""中国轮滑城"。

亚洲轮滑联合会授予其

"亚洲轮滑杰出贡献奖"。

The Beidaihe Roller Skating Festival has been held consecutively 20 times since 2005, becoming the largest roller skating festival event in the world. Beidaihe has been honored with titles such as "World Roller Skating Capital" and "China Roller Skating City" by the International Roller-skating Federation and the China Roller Skate Association. The World Skate Asia awarded it the "Outstanding Contribution to Asian Roller Sports" honor.

秦皇岛大力推动冰雪"三进"，
积极开展"万名中小学生冰雪体验活动"
"学校、机关、企业冰雪项目联赛"
"青少年冰雪冬令营"等赛事活动。
每年开展持续近 3 个月的
"秦皇岛之冬·欢乐冰雪季"系列活动，
趣味冰雪运动会、
迎新春滑雪挑战赛、
越野滑雪比赛等赛事活动异彩纷呈。

Qinhuangdao is vigorously promoting the "Three Advances" of winter sports, which refers to advancing ice and snow activities into government institutions, enterprises, and schools. The city actively organizes events such as the "Ten Thousand Students Ice and Snow Experience Program", the "School, Government, and Enterprise Winter Sports League", and the "Youth Winter Sports Camp". Each year, the city hosts the nearly three-month-long "Qinhuangdao Winter·Joyful Ice and Snow Season", featuring a variety of exciting activities. These include the Fun Winter Sports Games, the New Year Ski Challenge, and Cross-Country Skiing Competitions, all of which add vibrant energy to the winter season.

秦皇岛自行车运动拥有深厚的群众基础。
这里良好的气候环境和道路设施，
为自行车运动的开展提供了良好的基础条件。
中国国家自行车队长期在此驻训、比赛，
促进了秦皇岛自行车运动水平的提升。

Qinhuangdao boasts a strong foundation for cycling, with its favorable
climate and well-developed road infrastructure providing excellent
conditions for the sport. The Chinese National Cycling Team has
long used the city as a training and competition base, significantly
elevating the level of cycling in Qinhuangdao.

秦皇岛建有英伦国际、龙腾骑士、英皇国际等马术俱乐部，

不仅提供专业的马术训练，

还有精彩的马术演出，

集住宿、餐饮、休闲、研学于一体，

成为度假休闲的好去处。

The city is also home to prestigious equestrian clubs such as British International, Longteng Knights, and Yinghuang International. These clubs not only offer professional equestrian training but also host captivating equestrian performances. Combining accommodations, dining, leisure, and educational activities, they have become premier destinations for vacationers and enthusiasts alike.

秦皇岛市网球联赛至今已举办 9 届。

组织者在赛事宣传、转播方面不断创新，

直播和短视频观看人数近千万，

已成为国内极具影响力的业余团体网球赛事之一。

The Qinhuangdao Tennis League has now successfully held nine editions. Organizers have continuously innovated in event promotion and broadcasting, with live streams and short videos attracting nearly 10 million viewers. The league has become one of the most influential amateur team tennis tournaments in China.

秦皇岛将铁人三项赛作为一张城市名片全力扶持和培育。

自 2006 年起已成功举办了 16 届铁人三项赛。

来自世界各地的"铁人"激烈角逐，

尽展不惧挑战、不言放弃的精神品质。

Qinhuangdao has embraced triathlon as a signature city event, providing strong support and nurturing its growth. Since 2006, the city has hosted 16 successful triathlon competitions. Athletes from around the globe have competed fiercely, embodying the indomitable spirit of embracing challenges and never giving up.

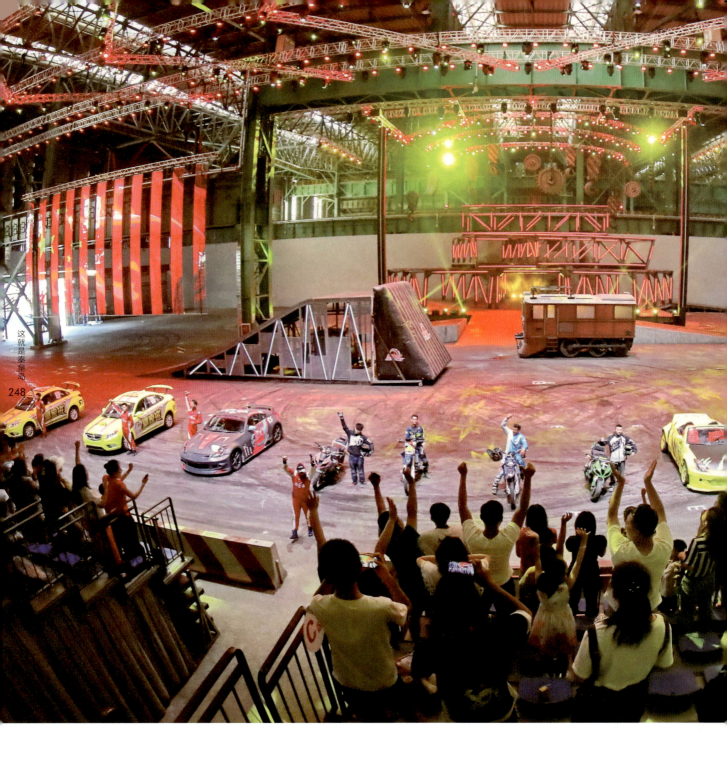

秦皇岛首钢赛车谷

是世界上第一条穿梭于钢铁工业区的街道赛赛道，

也是中国首个保护和利用工业遗产的街道赛赛道。

这里先后承办了 CEC 中国汽车耐力锦标赛、

速度中国北方汽车系列赛、

米其林竞驰 GPGP 金港大奖赛、

京津冀赛车节等一系列重要赛事。

Qinhuangdao Shougang Racing Valley is the world's first street racing circuit that weaves through a steel industrial area and is also China's first street racing circuit dedicated to the protection and utilization of industrial heritage. It has hosted events such as the China Endurance Championship(CEC), Northern China Speed, Michelin Pilot Sport Golden Port Grand Prix, and the Beijing-Tianjin-Hebei Racing Festival.

这里是莘莘学子的科研热土

A Hub for Academic Research

秦皇岛拥有 12 所高等院校、

351 家科技创新平台，

人才密度和万人有效发明专利拥有量

均居河北省首位。

Qinhuangdao is home to 12 higher education institutions and 351 technology innovation platforms, ranking first in Hebei Province in terms of talent density and the number of effective invention patents per 10,000 people.

燕山大学是全国重点大学，

源于哈尔滨工业大学，

始建于 1920 年，

1960 年独立办学。

1985 年至 1997 年，学校整体南迁至秦皇岛。

学校设有研究生院和 18 个直属学院，

73 个本科专业，

12 个博士后流动站，

14 个博士学位一级学科。

Yanshan University is a nationally recognized key university. It has its origins in the Harbin Institute of Technology, which was established in 1920, became independent in 1960, and relocated entirely to Qinhuangdao from 1985 to 1997. It comprises a graduate school, 18 directly affiliated colleges, 73 undergraduate programs, 12 post-doctoral research stations, and 14 first-level doctoral disciplines.

东北大学秦皇岛分校

是东北大学的重要组成部分，

设有东北大学研究生院秦皇岛分院、

1 个中外合作办学机构和 8 个学院，

37 个本科专业，

共享东北大学全部博士和硕士学科点资源。

Northeast University at Qinhuangdao is an integral part of Northeast University. It includes the Northeast University Graduate School at Qinhuangdao, one Sino-foreign cooperative educational institution, and 8 colleges, offering 37 undergraduate programs and sharing all doctoral and master's degree programs with Northeast University.

亚稳材料制备技术与科学国家重点实验室

是依托燕山大学建设的国家重点实验室，

是河北省唯一的学科类国家重点实验室，

以亚稳材料制备技术与科学为主题，

立足于基础和应用基础研究，

同时注重向应用开发延伸。

该实验室的

田永君教授于 2017 年当选中国科学院院士，

刘日平教授于 2023 年当选中国工程院院士。

The State Key Laboratory of Metastable Materials Science and Technology is a national key laboratory established with the support of Yanshan University. It is the only discipline-based national key laboratory in Hebei Province, focusing on the technology and science of metastable material preparation. The laboratory emphasizes both fundamental and applied basic research, with a strong focus on extending towards applied development. Professor Tian Yongjun, affiliated with this laboratory, was elected as an academician of the Chinese Academy of Sciences in 2017, and Professor Liu Riping was elected as an academician of the Chinese Academy of Engineering in 2023.

这里是中老年人的康养福地

A Wellness Haven for Middle-Aged and Elderly People

|北京大学第三医院秦皇岛医院 |
| Peking University Third Hospital Qinhuangdao Hospital |

秦皇岛加快建设国家区域医疗中心，

北京大学第三医院秦皇岛医院、

北京中医药大学东方医院秦皇岛医院、

天津市肿瘤医院秦皇岛医院

三大国家区域医疗中心项目先后落地。

大力推进培疗机构改革，

推广"医养康深度融合"

"城企联动普惠养老服务"模式，

成为秦皇岛一张崭新亮丽名片。

Qinhuangdao is accelerating the construction of National Regional Medical Centers. Key projects such as Peking University Third Hospital Qinhuangdao Hospital, Beijing University of Chinese Medicine Dongfang Hospital Qinhuangdao Hospital, and Tianjin Cancer Hospital Qinhuangdao Hospital have been established successively. The city is vigorously advancing reforms in healthcare and elderly care institutions, promoting models like the "deep integration of medical care, elderly care, and health preservation" and the "city-enterprise collaborative model for inclusive elderly care services", making these initiatives a bright new hallmark of Qinhuangdao.

秦皇岛拥有 55 家养老机构，

其中 30 家为医养结合的养老机构，

正致力于打造一个让老年人

老有所养、老有所乐的康养名城。

中国康养恒颐汇是中国康养首个医养结合项目，

也是河北省机构养老的标杆项目。

此外，秦皇岛还建设了康复辅助器具产业园区，

引进康复辅助器具研发、制造、检测配置项目，

并延伸做好康复服务、养生养老事业，

用有爱的康复辅具呵护无碍的幸福生活。

Qinhuangdao has 55 elderly care institutions, including 30 that integrate medical care with elderly care, striving to build a renowned wellness city where the elderly can be well-cared for and enjoy their lives. China Health and Elderly Care Hengyihui is China's first integrated medical and elderly care project and serves as a benchmark for institutional elderly care in Hebei Province. In addition, Qinhuangdao has established a Rehabilitation Assistive Devices Industrial Park, introduced projects for the research, development, manufacturing, and testing of rehabilitation assistive devices, and tended to provide excellent rehabilitation services and promote wellness and elderly care. Loving rehabilitation assistive devices are used to nurture a barrier-free and happy life.

这里有吃货老饕的美食盛宴

A Seafood Feast for Gourmets

穿行在秦皇岛的大街小巷，

仿佛置身于"舌尖上的中国"实景拍摄地。

浓郁的烟火气萦绕其间，

让你的嗅觉和味蕾全方位得到满足，

那回味无穷的滋味更让广大游客流连忘返。

Walking through Qinhuangdao's streets and alleys is like stepping into the filming locations of "A Bite of China", with a rich, aromatic atmosphere that satisfies both your sense of smell and taste. The unforgettable flavors leave visitors lingering for more.

到地道海鲜小馆，

品尝海滨城市新鲜的海鲜大餐。

You can visit authentic seafood restaurants to savor fresh seafood feasts in this coastal city.

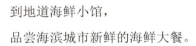

Delicious food

到街头巷尾，

探访山海关浑锅、

北戴河杨肠子、

卢龙扒猪脸等当地特色美食。

You can explore the streets to discover local specialties such as Shanhaiguan Hun Guo (mixed hotpot), Beidaihe Yangchangzi Sausage, and Lulong Pork Head.

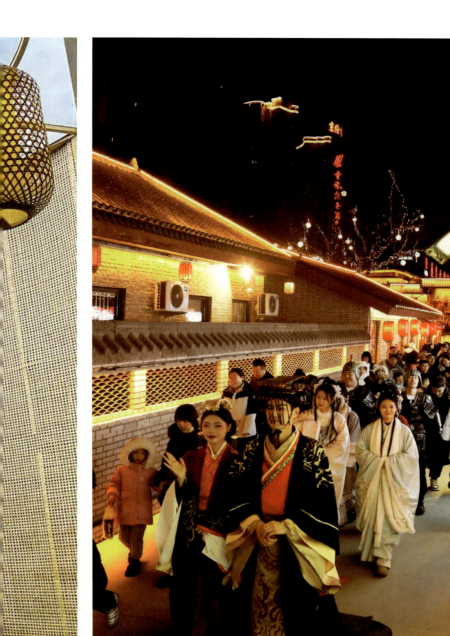

到秦皇小巷美食街，
感受最抚凡人心的小巷烟火气。

You can head to Qinhuang Alley Food Street to experience the comforting and homely atmosphere of the narrow alleyways.

到葡萄小镇、红酒庄园，

欣赏葡园风光，

感受红酒文化，

体验葡萄美酒的香醇。

Visit the Grape Town and Chateau Kings Wellness Manor to admire the vineyard landscapes, immerse yourself in the culture of winemaking, and savor the rich flavors of fine wines.

秦皇岛是中国第一瓶干红葡萄酒的诞生地，现已形成华夏长城、茅台、香格里拉、朗格斯、地王、金士、海亚湾柳河山庄、仁轩等高端葡萄酒酿造企业集群。

Qinhuangdao holds the distinction of being the birthplace of China's first bottle of dry redwine. Today, it has developed a cluster of premium winemaking enterprises, including Huaxia Great Wall, Moutai, Shangri-La, Langgs, Diwang, Kings, Liuhe Vineyard, and Renxuan, solidifying its reputation as a hub for high-quality wine production.

北戴河牌赤霞珠干红葡萄酒于 1984 年荣获
"轻工业部酒类评比大赛"金杯奖。

Beidaihe Brand Cabernet Sauvignon Dry Red
Wine, was honored with the Gold Cup Award at the
1984 National Wine Competition organized by the
Ministry of Light Industry.

邂逅秦皇岛，

你会发现这座人文厚重、山海壮美、

个性独特的城市发生着深刻的变革，

她于探索中重构着北方海滨城市旅游

和新兴工业协同发展的新模式，

正在寻求创新、协调、绿色、开放、共享的

平衡发展道路，那条希望之路。

今天的秦皇岛古老而又年轻，

她的魅力持久并且立体。

她向你展开邀约的手臂，

愿与你一起书写更加美好的未来长卷！

Encountering Qinhuangdao, you will discover a city rich in culture, majestic in her mountains and seas, and uniquely characterized by profound transformations. Through exploration, she has pioneered a new model of simultaneous development in tourism in northern coastal cities and emerging industries, seeking a balanced path of innovative, coordinated, green, open and shared development—the path of hope. Today's Qinhuangdao is both ancient and youthful, with a lasting and multidimensional charm. she extends an inviting hand, hoping to join you in writing an even more beautiful future together!

后记
POSTSCRIPT

随着《这就是秦皇岛》缓缓合上，相信各位读者朋友已经对秦皇岛进行了一次视觉与心灵的旅行，身临其境地感受到了这座海滨城市美丽又深邃、蓬勃又诗意的迷人特质。

一提起秦皇岛，大家就会想到这里是旅游城市，是休闲度假胜地，但现今的秦皇岛要更立体，更丰富多彩。秦皇岛市丁伟市长接受《财经》杂志采访时谈道，秦皇岛正发生着深刻变革，按照新发展理念要求，既要绿水青山，又要金山银山，既做软性服务业，又做高端制造和战略性新兴产业，这是高起点、高效益、高附加值的城市产业定位，也是北方滨海城市旅游与高新技术产业协同发展的新模式。我们循着这一思路及近年秦皇岛改革发展实践，策划并组织编著了这本书。衷心希望本书能引领您走进秦皇岛如画的碧海金沙，见证她蝶变的产业集群，领略她璀璨的人间烟火。

本书编印过程中，从资料搜集到落笔成文，从图片征集到现场拍摄，从设计排版到印刷制作，得到了市政府办公室、市发改委、市工信局、市旅游文广局、市体育局、开发区管委等单位，以及燕山大学出版社、秦皇岛日报社、秦皇岛市摄影家协会和相关企业的大力支持，在此深表谢意。同时，也向所有参与本书策划的同人、所有为本书提供图片的摄影家、所有为本书付出辛勤劳动的编辑致敬，是你们的支持与付出，让这份关于秦皇岛的美好得以呈现。

今日的秦皇岛，正以前所未有的速度和热情，拥抱世界，迈向未来。感谢每一位翻阅这本书的读者朋友，是您的关注与支持，给予了我们不断前行的动力。秦皇岛诚挚向您邀约，期待与您相遇，欢迎您来共同书写这座城市的美好故事。

编者

2024 年 12 月 30 日